Missing Presumed Drowned

A true story of the internment of Italians resident in Britain during the Second World War

Stefano Paolini

Published by Stefano Paolini

Published by Stefano Paolini

ISBN 978-0-9933121-0-6

To Mum, Dad and Nonna

Stefano Paolini is a second-generation British Italian. His father is from Tuscany and his mother from Emilia-Romagna. A former car mechanic and voice-over artist, a Sport Science graduate and currently a stand-up comedian, Stefano was born and raised in Brixton, South London. *Missing Presumed Drowned* is his debut book.

Contents

.

Acknowledgements

This book would not have been possible without the following people, and I would like to give thanks to Angela Albericci, Rando Bertoia, Bruna Bonino, Albert Cavalli, Armo Collini, Clementina Cordani, Liliana Cortesio, Graziella Feraboli (who appears on the front cover with her father, Ettore, in a photo taken in the 1930s), Harold Finney, Peter Foster, Rupert Limentani, Frank Longinotti, Vito Maestranzi, Maria Moruzzi, Rita Pezzani, Joe Pieri, Fosca Rendina, Johnny Sidoli, Aurelio Tarquini, Alfred Tisi and Dino (Andrea) Viazzani for allowing me into their homes to be interviewed, or corresponding with me through the post. A special thank you to Graziella Feraboli, whose story inspired me to write this book.

I would like to thank Maria Serena Balestracci and Terri Colpi for their help locating primary sources of information. My work has benefitted greatly from their generosity and kindness. I would like to thank St Peters Italian Church in Clarkenwell, the Scalabrini Centre in Brixton and Beppe Conti in Bardi for their help in locating and contacting contributors. Thankyou to Hugh Alexander at the National Archive at Kew, the archivist at Bury Library in Greater Manchester, and Tudor Allen at the Camden Local Studies and Archives Centre. Thanks to Alfio Bernabei, Alan Davis and Angelo Iudice, at Accademia Apulia UK. I would like to apologise for any omisissions that I might have made regarding the research of the book.

I would like to thank Wendy Toole for helping me with the primary and secondary drafts and Sara Donaldson for helping me in the final stage with proof reading. Their professionalism and eye for detail has been fantastic. Special thanks to Juliette Norsworthy, for creating the amazing design for the front and back covers.
Huge thanks to my friends for taking an interest in my, work, especially Julia Chamberlain and Katherine Webb.

Finally, I would like to thank my family for all their love and support, not just when I was researching and writing Missing Presumed Drowned, but during everything I have decided to do in my life. Thank you.

Preface

Britain and Italy are countries that have played a significant role in my life. Italy is the birthplace of my parents and Britain is my birthplace. As a second-generation British Italian, I have the sense that I am not entirely British or Italian. This feeling of acceptance by, and at the same time alienation from, both countries stems from the perceptions that institutions and people in general have in their minds of where I'm from. The British government regards me as British and has issued me a British passport, as has the Italian government. Many people in Britain regard me as Italian and many people in Italy regard me as British. Is it my blood or my birthplace that decides where I'm from?

Questions of allegiance and identity are common especially during occasions of heightened patriotism such as sporting competitions and tournaments. Who do you support? It's a difficult question to answer because I don't want to seem ungrateful or to offend either side by picking one country over the other. I have been fortunate enough to grow up and live in an age where these questions are confined to the theatre of sport. However, for thousands of

British Italians in Britain during the 1940s these perceptions and questions of allegiance and identity reached the far higher seriousness of the theatre of war.

For a period during the Second World War, between June 1940 and September 1943, Britain and Italy were at war with each other. In the eyes of the British government 25,000 or so British Italians were enemy aliens. The question of allegiance and identity was not a matter for discussion. Internment was put into effect by the British government as a defence measure, and the entire Italian male population resident in Britain at the time was arrested without charge and detained indefinitely without trial.

Several hundred were deported to British dominions abroad, which led to one of the largest disasters for allied shipping in the entire war. *Missing Presumed Drowned* is about this episode of the Second World War and its effects on the home front.

Writing a non-fiction book about an event that happened 75 years ago is fraught with challenges and difficulties, not least that of sorting fact from fiction and fact from propaganda. In this respect I have been fortunate that many of the people impacted by the defence measure were alive at the time of writing and were willing to be interviewed. Therefore the narrative of the book is in part based upon first-hand accounts of people who were interned. Where first-hand accounts were unavailable, second-hand accounts from relatives of internees were used. Documents from the National Archive, newspaper articles from the period and books written on the subject at the time and after the Second World War were used to put the stories into their historical context. For many former internees and their relatives, speaking to me was the first time they had openly talked about their experiences as enemy aliens during the war.

Missing Presumed Drowned is not the first book written on the subject but is a small contribution to a very slim body of work. There are only a handful of publications specifically written about the defence measure and its impact on the people of Italian origin in Britain, so it is hoped that *Missing Presumed Drowned* will not be the last. Although it was a defence measure used to protect Britain from a possible invasion from within, it has yet to reach the public consciousness in the way that other defence measures implemented at the same time have. The aim of this book is to document and present the stories of those whom that the measure affected. A terrible tragedy befell the British Italian community all those years ago. An even greater tragedy would be for it to be forgotten completely.

1

British Italians

In September 1939, Graziella Feraboli was 14 years old. She was born in Britain to Italian parents and lived with her mother and father in Clapham, south-west London. Her father, Ettore, was born in Cremona, in Lombardy, and was a professional violinist. Her mother, Tina Morini, was born in Florence, in Tuscany, and was a pianist who accompanied singers and instrumentalists. After the First World War, Ettore decided to go to London because he was having trouble finding work in Cremona and he had heard through friends of colleagues that there were opportunities for him in his profession. So he left Italy for London, and it wasn't long before he got a job and settled there.

Tina, on the other hand, was from an established family in Florence and her parents didn't take kindly to the idea of her going to London. This did not dissuade her, however, and under the guise of visiting some friends who lived in the city she set off. She stayed with her friends for a while, but she fell in love with London and London life, the

British culture and language, and the freedom of London away from the restrictions of her middle-class life in Florence.

Like Ettore, Tina found opportunities in her profession and she became an accompanist. It was one evening, during a concert in which Ettore and Tina were both professionally engaged, that they met, explained Graziella:

> I suppose they must have fallen in love, and they married, and they both decided to settle and remain in London. They married and that's where I was born. They bought a house in south-west London [Clapham]. We were a very happy family, with two Italian parents and one British-born daughter. It was a very interesting life because they both were extremely busy people. My father played for his profession continuously, my mother taught a lot as well as accompanying, so the house was lively, full of people going in and out, lots of music – not that it was an easy life. It was hard work – they were professional people who worked very hard.[1]

At five years of age, Graziella was able to read and write in Italian. Wanting her to be fluent in the language, her parents delayed her entry into school by a year and at the age of six she went to La Retraite Catholic School for Girls in south-west London. She had a good grasp of English, too, and integrated well into her new school:

> I was very happy indeed. I was never made to feel different, although I had a rather unpronounceable name, and black hair; I spoke and behaved like an English person. If anything, the fact of the 'Italianness' was a sort of distinctive feature, which made me very proud of being two things at the same time. It was very pleasant to know that I had two backgrounds, two languages.[2]

Ettore, Tina and Graziella were three people from a population of around 25,000 Italians resident in Britain in the late 1930s, the majority from the areas of Italy known as Ciociaria and Tuscany and the northern region of Emilia-Romagna. Before post-war immigration from Commonwealth countries such as Jamaica, India and Pakistan, Italians were one of the largest groups of immigrants in urban areas in Britain. They were first-, second-, third- and fourth-generation immigrants who had made Britain their home. Some families could trace their ancestors back as far as the 1850s and 1860s, which was the start of the period that saw large numbers of Italians from northern Italy emigrating to Germany, France, America and Britain. Through the middle of the nineteenth and the early part of the twentieth century, Italian communities became established in urban areas in Britain. The first 'Little Italy' was in Clerkenwell, London, and as Italians made their way north, a 'Little Italy' formed in the Ancoats area of Manchester.

Giovanni Longinotti was born in Santa Maria del Taro, Emilia-Romagna, in 1892. Following in the family footsteps, he left northern Italy and emigrated to the north of England to work in a family-run ice cream business belonging to an uncle of his. Giovanni sold ice cream from a horse-drawn cart in Ancoats. He eventually married a British woman of Italian heritage from the same town, whose parents were also in the ice cream trade. The couple had two children, one of whom was Frank, born in Manchester on 1 September 1928.

When Frank and his brother were babies, Giovanni and Tina moved the family to Haywood in Greater Manchester. Giovanni continued making and selling ice cream, one of only a few Italians in Heywood to do so, and after a few years became well known in the area. His wife stayed at home to look after the boys until they had finished school and were old enough to join the family business.

Selling ice cream in a small town was a sociable enterprise and meant that Giovanni was in contact with the people of the area, and the local children would flock round his cart. Indeed, most of the customers were children, as Frank recalled: 'My father could ramble off children's names one after the other ... he would get to know them. [It was a] very pleasant job really, you know, the ice cream.'[3]

The ice cream factory was at the back of the family house. The horses were kept in a stable behind the local pub that the landlord had no use for. One of the horses was called Prince and the other, a piebald, was called Tommy. The people in the town knew the cart was arriving by the sound that the iron wheels made as it was pulled through the streets, and the horses and cart made quite a spectacle as both were decorated. The back of the cart was closed but the sides would open to serve customers, and ice cream was very popular in the summer especially during carnivals and at parties and weddings. The ice cream was kept cold by ice stored in barrows under the tubs of ice cream, and the price was a penny for either vanilla or lemon. Italians dominated the ice cream trade. There were hundreds of ice cream carts up and down the country, with Italian icemen supplying ice from Norway to freeze the confectionery.

Other Italians went to Scotland and settled in Glasgow and Edinburgh. Joe Pieri was born in Barga, Tuscany. A year after the armistice that ended the First World War, when Joe was one year old, he was taken to Scotland by his father. After being demobbed from the Italian army, Joe's father couldn't find work in Barga but a local priest told him that there was a city called Glasgow, to the north of Britain, and that Italians there were looking for workers. His father packed his belongings and together with Joe's brother and mother went to Glasgow.

As well as being ice cream sellers and ice merchants, Italians were opening fish and chip shops. While Joe was growing up and going to school, his father began working as a helper in one such shop:

I left school at the age of 13 or 14 because that was the expected thing to do, you had to go and help the family. So by this time my father had bought the shop he originally worked in when he first came to Glasgow, and together with my brother and mother the four of us worked in the shop and we became reasonably prosperous.[4]

Fish and chips shops were popular in Scotland, but in Wales it was temperance bars. The temperance movement in Wales served Italians well, and hundreds of family-run shops were opened in the Welsh Valleys and towns. Serving ice cream, lemonade and sarsaparilla in the summer, and hot pork pies and Oxo in the winter, Italians like Clementina Cordani's father, Ernie, were able to prosper there. Ernie had emigrated from Grezzo, a hamlet of Bardi, in Emilia-Romagna, in February 1920, as a 16-year-old boy:

He had never been outside of Bardi, never seen a train before. It took him three days to come to Great Britain and I think there were five or six young boys all coming to work in Aberdaye [Wales].[5]

Once Ernie had established himself, he returned to Grezzo, married and started a family. As was a common practice in those days, the family stayed in Italy and he returned to Wales to work. Families would join their men later, as in Clementina's case. She was born in Grezzo in 1933 and went to Wales in 1939.

As well as opening up small family-run catering businesses, Italians also made careers as middle managers in the some of the most well known restaurants and hotels in the West End of London. Cesare Maggi, for example, was restaurant manager at the Ritz Hotel. One of London's prominent hot spots for dance music in the 1930s was the Monseigneur Restaurant, a fashionable London diner that featured cabaret performances. Along with the Savoy and the Mayfair Hotel, it was a top showcase for the popular music of the day. Its chef and restaurant manager were both Italians resident in London, as were the restaurant managers of the Savoy and the Mayfair Hotel. It was fashionable and desirable at that time for West End restaurants to be managed and staffed by Italian waiters, and such was the popularity of Italian catering services that a second 'Little Italy' became established in London's Soho district, formed of cafés, restaurants and provisions stores.

Up until the late nineteenth century, the main restriction on Italians gaining entry into Britain was the cost of the journey. However, laws on immigration were passed at the start of the twentieth century, with the Aliens Act in 1905 and the Aliens Restriction (Amendment) Act in 1919. The laws had little impact on Italian immigration and were passed mainly to curb large-scale immigration of Jews from Russia to the East End of London, which was blamed for the increase in squalor in the area. New immigrants had to show staff at immigration that they had means of sustaining themselves, had accommodation and were not criminals. The 1919 Act passed after the First World War gave the government further powers to control alien entry.

Prior to this Act the British government held few records of Italians in Britain, though around 100 years of immigration had already occurred. The Italians had come from poverty and built wealth through hard work and family values. They now owned businesses and houses, and had set up schools, churches, hospitals and social clubs. They suffered some discrimination and intolerance – their dark features highlighted their racial difference, and their Catholic religion caused tension in some areas – but on the whole they were well integrated into British life and accepted by both their neighbours and the British government. Some Italians had been taken to Britain by their parents as babies and had grown up there, and hundreds of children were born in Britain to Italian parents, which meant that they had dual citizenship. British women married Italian men and took their nationality. There didn't seem to be much difference between being an alien or being a British citizen, and indeed this difference had no significance prior to the Second World War.

Being an alien meant that you could live and work in Britain. You might be an Italian alien but speak with a Scottish, Welsh, northern, cockney or 'received pronunciation' accent. However, being an alien meant that you didn't enjoy the same rights regarding property and employment as a British citizen with whom you shared a culture and an accent. For example, enforcing the Aliens Restriction (Amendment) Act of 1919, the government could force aliens to register with the police, requisition their property, force employers to sack them and repossess their homes. Under certain conditions, the government could even intern and deport aliens if they were perceived to be members of a subversive organisation.

From very humble origins Italians had been able to work their way into environments that they would not otherwise have had access to. In 1939, first- and second-generation Italians seemed to have everything in Britain. But it was all built on the foundation of alien status, and in the right circumstances it could all be taken away from them. Storm clouds were gathering over Europe, and a community that had spent several decades in their adopted country were in a perilous position.

2

The Second World War

In August 1939 the spectre of war loomed large. The Home, Foreign and War offices, along with the Admiralty, were preparing Britain for war. In August 1939, Peter Foster was 20 years of age and holidaying on the SS *Arandora Star*, a cruise ship run by Blue Star Line Limited. The cruise was cut short, as Peter described:

> We set sail for Helsinki, and that was one of the great times of one's life because four o' clock one afternoon we were having tea and suddenly the ship turned around and then the Tannoy came on for us all to hear from the captain saying 'the Admiralty has ordered the *Arandora Star* back to Southampton'; we all thought, well, this may be the beginning of something, and indeed it was. Next morning we were steaming back through the Baltic and every morning a little aeroplane flew around the ship – it had a swastika on it, and this kept up until we got to Southampton. We knew or we guessed what was going to happen – everybody was getting ready for war – and then we happily disembarked.[1]

On 1 September 1939 Germany invaded Poland, with a devastating combination of air and ground offences called 'blitzkrieg'. Britain and France gave Germany an ultimatum to withdraw its troops from Poland. The ultimatum was not met, and on 3 September the British government declared war on Germany. Peter Foster went to Scotland to join the sappers; the Master of the *Arandora Star*, Edgar Wallace Moulton, and her crew awaited their orders from the Admiralty and its First Lord, Winston Churchill, who had joined the War Cabinet on 3 September, returning to the post he had held during the First World War.

Following the declaration of war, borders were closed and people abroad were left stranded. In the summer of that year Graziella Feraboli and her mother had gone to visit relatives in Italy; Ettore had remained in London to work. After the borders were closed they were unable to return to Britain and instead stayed with relatives in Florence until they obtained a visa some months later:

> We crossed France in a blacked-out train, crossed the Channel and got back to London. That was a shock because all of a sudden I knew life was not going to be the

same as before. We got off the train at Victoria station, blackout – never seen a blackout in my life before – and a very sombre atmosphere. I could feel that the situation was serious. Gas masks all over the place, balloons in the sky ... it was a totally different London.[2]

Although Graziella, Ettore and Tina were delighted to see one another again, the city of London was on high alert. The BBC had closed down its regional services and reduced them to one single synchronised output, broadcasting information and instructions in preparation for war.

The Second World War would be a war like no other before it. Unlike the First World War, where the front line was many miles away in a foreign country, mass mechanised artillery such as aeroplane bombers, piloted by men whose instructions were to destroy the cities of the enemy, brought the front line immediately to the British civilian population. Aerial bombardment had razed Warsaw, the Polish capital, to the ground, with huge loss of civilian life. In anticipation, the British government, under Prime Minister Neville Chamberlain, implemented defence measures. To minimise the risk of a single bomb causing mass casualties, gatherings of large numbers of people in public places were banned, including at football matches and musical events. This may have had an impact on Ettore's work, but he had other problems to concern himself with.

There was mass evacuation from urban areas with high-density populations, and relocation to the countryside. The most vulnerable, such as pregnant women, children, the disabled and the elderly, were uprooted, and by the start of September around 1.5 million people had been moved from British cities to safer areas. Entire schools were moved together with their teachers. Ettore and Tina followed the instructions of the British authorities and prepared a suitcase of belongings for Graziella: 'Within days my mother packed me off to my new school in Portsmouth,'[3] she recalled.

Ettore and Tina were fortunate enough to know where Graziella had been sent, but this was not the case for all parents. Speed was of the essence; the bombers could arrive at any moment. Such was the haste to implement the measure that many parents only knew of their child's final destination when they received a postcard from them with a contact address.

Bruna Bonino was born in London in 1925. Her Italian family ran a café in Cock Lane near Smithfield's meat market. Her two younger brothers, Tony and Carlo, were evacuated from the area and the family received news of their location when they arrived at Wootton Bassett near Swindon. Separation of siblings was commonplace in a policy where haste was paramount and available space in family homes limited. However, Tony and Carlo remained together, as Bruna explained:

> Tony was crying so much to be with his brother that they
> had to find a family that would take the two of them.
> They ended up at a dairy in the country. We used to send
> parcels and clothes, and when we went down there, my
> mum and me, my Carlo would come up to me and say,
> 'Why don't you come down here every day?'[4]

Initially, the bombers that the government were expecting in September 1939 did not appear. They would arrive the following year, during the Blitz. However, the German generals used a different tactic to sap the strength of the British war effort. Britain was a country that relied on imports to feed its population, and it was on the high seas that the Germans concentrated their attack. British ships carrying cargo across the Atlantic from America and Canada were relentlessly attacked by U-boats. From September 1939 to May 1940 a total of 268 ships, ranging from battleships to trawlers, were sunk. Between May and December 1940, 57 ships were lost each month.

Such was the extent of the losses that food rationing was introduced in January 1940. This meant that British households would have to make do with less. Rationing imposed restrictions on catering businesses, too. The arrival of the war put an end to the manufacture of ice cream altogether because some of the ingredients were rationed: 'The war broke out, rationing came in and stuff like ice cream was banned because of the sugar that they used,'[5] said Frank Longinotti. His father Giovanni went into the fish and chip trade instead. As well as sugar and cheese, meat was rationed, and often Italian knife grinders found their services no longer required. Many in this profession were from the Trentino part of Italy and had been some of the earliest Italian arrivals in Britain; they passed their skills from generation to generation. Armo Collini's grandfather and father were knife grinders whose work started to dry out but they found new contracts. 'He [Dad] sharpened knives for government canteens, essential work, butchers and that,'[6] said Armo. The family had to resort to doing the job by hand as petrol was rationed and they could no longer use their motorised van.

For café and restaurant owners and managers, rations were calculated on the number of meals they had been serving before rationing was introduced. In the West End, Italian restaurant managers like Cesare Maggi at the Ritz Hotel and banqueting manager Ettore Zavattoni at the Savoy had to adapt fine dining within the limits of rationing.

After following a policy of appeasement for many years, the British government found their army to be inadequate in size against the army of Germany, whose government had followed a policy of rearmament. On 3 September, the British government passed the National Service Act, which enforced conscription of all British males aged between 18 and 41 years of age resident in the United Kingdom. In households across Britain, second-generation

Italians received notification that they were being conscripted.

Tranquillo Tarchetti was born in Italy in 1872. Little is known about his early years, but by 1911 he had emigrated from Italy to Britain and had married Annie, a British subject from Ashford in Kent, who became Italian through her marriage to him. The couple had four children, including Pietro Lluellyn Gordon Tarchetti, born around 1909 in London. In 1911 the family lived in Lambeth; Tranquillo was a restaurant waiter and Annie a registered midwife. By 1939 Tranquillo and Annie were living in Mersham, near to Annie's birthplace in Kent. When war broke out their son Pietro was in his thirties and was conscripted into the 9th Battalion Cameronians (Scottish Rifles), based in Glasgow. He served as a rifleman, using the anglicised version of his name, Peter. The battalion was raised that year and formed part of the UK defensive force.

At the same time, the government was issuing instructions in newspapers and on the radio for aliens to register with the police. Italians accordingly made their way to their local police stations to register their details and pay a registration fee. After completing the relevant forms, they received their alien registration certificates. These certificates gave details of name, address, marital status and employment and included a photograph. As the war progressed, new aliens fleeing Nazi persecution arrived in Britain from Germany and Austria.

At the start of the war, the British government had made plans for interning aliens who were deemed to pose a threat to the security of the country. The responsibility for drawing up the lists fell to MI5, and members of organisations that were viewed as subversive were at the top of it. German nationals who were members of the Nazi party, and were either resident in Britain or in Britain at the time, were interned immediately at the outbreak of hostilities. They numbered around 500 people. However, there were also thousands of German and Austrian Jewish refugees entering and seeking sanctuary in Britain. Wary that among the alien refugees the Germans would try to smuggle spies to sabotage the British war effort, Neville Chamberlain's government held tribunals as a counter measure to the threat.

Around 73,000 individuals, mainly Germans and Austrians, were given tribunals between September 1939 and May 1940 and graded 'A', 'B' or 'C'. The assumption that an individual was innocent until proven guilty was reversed, and it was up to the alien to prove his or her innocence. The grading determined their destiny. Grade 'A' faced immediate internment, grade 'B' faced restrictions on movements and possessions while grade 'C' faced no restrictions. Several hundred were categorised as 'A' at the start of the war and some 7,000 were categorised as 'B', but the majority, around 60,000, were categorised as 'C'. Many in this group were women, children and the elderly.

MI5 had also compiled a list of Italians who would be interned immediately if Italy entered into the war against Britain. The lists comprised names of 1,200 resident Italians who lived in England, Scotland, Wales and Northern Ireland and 300 British-born Italians also resident in Britain. The lists were made up of Italians who were members of the *fascio*. MI5 rated these men as category 'A', the same as German aliens who were members of the Nazi party and viewed as posing the greatest threat to Britain; they would be the first to be arrested if Italy declared war.

Italian Fascism in Britain

In 1940 Italy was a country with a fascist government that had been in office for 19 years. After taking power in 1921 with a march on Rome, Benito Mussolini became Italy's Prime Minister and later dictator. In his earlier years Mussolini had been a socialist, the editor of a left-wing magazine and a one-time recruit of the British security services during the First World War. He was well paid to promote the Italian war effort in his magazine when many in Italy wanted out. However, the First World War and what Mussolini experienced as a corporal serving in the Italian army altered his political views, and fascism (a political doctrine that encouraged the corporate state and nationalism) was born.

However, Italy would have to overcome vast differences within the parochial mind-set of a population united in name but little else for his vision to be realised. It was common for people in the north and south of Italy to speak different dialects, with little understanding of each other and even less in common. Italian émigrés were also included in Mussoloni's movement, and so it was that a community in Britain that had been established since the 1850s had its first involvement with Italian fascism.

The *fascio* in London was established in 1921. It was one of the first such groups to be founded outside Italy and was visited by Mussolini in 1922. Count Dino Grandi was appointed as the fascist Italian Ambassador and was the perfect man for the job. Unlike his predecessors, he was often found among the Italians in social situations and this gave him an approachability and accessibility within the community that helped to sell the party. A range of social and cultural activities were organised, and as membership grew, so did the *fascio*. By 1940 it had moved from Greek Street to Charing Cross Road, and the Casa del Littorio was founded. In Roman times the Casa del Littorio was the building from where a Roman magistrate would enforce Roman laws across the empire. The modern Littorio was symbolic of those past days, rather than having actual power.

The grand new headquarters of the *fascio* was closer to London's second 'Little Italy' in Soho than to the original 'Little Italy' in Clerkenwell. St Peter's Church was the epicentre of that first 'Little Italy', the church being the focal point of the early Italian community. The second 'Little Italy' had come about later and was based in a prosperous economic area. Religion was not a prominent feature of fascist ideology, and the new centre for Italians in London sent out the message that the new way was better than the old. Italians were no longer living in the slums but in the splendour of the West End. They were encouraged to embrace politics rather than religion and to replace parochialism with nationalism.

In its growth from a few members to several thousand, the organisation incorporated into one movement a large number of associations that Italians had started in London before the arrival of fascism. The clubhouse in Charing Cross Road was the focal point and served several important functions, in that the building housed the administrative headquarters of the Italian schools situated throughout London. Rooms were used for Italian classes and also accommodated a school for young musicians, especially violinists. There was an after-work club, a women's section, and a number of social events such as dinner dances.

By 1939 there were 11 Italian schools in London with 1,300 students, mostly the British-born offspring of Italian immigrants. Reaching out to the second generation was important, and children were encouraged to join the Balilla, a youth movement that encouraged the militarisation of fascism. The movement had its own newspaper, *L'Italia Nostra* ('Our Italy'), and a holiday house at Felixstowe.

The strength of the movement lay in utilising Italians established in London rather than sending over delegates from Italy who would have poor knowledge of the people and local life. The movement harnessed the skills of those who were already actively promoting Italian interests within the community. Graziella Feraboli's parents, Ettore and Tina, were two such Italians whose skills were employed:

> The Italian consul [Dino Grandi] at the time, who knew my mother, asked her if she would undertake to open up the first school for Italian children in London because she was a qualified teacher – this she did, and she was

enthusiastic about the idea. Children who lived in homes where they only heard dialect spoken were able to learn to read and write in Italian and also learn about Italy, its culture, its geography, and its history and so on ... My father worked sometimes with the Casa del Littorio, where he had his studio and was teaching violin to a large number of students, young people – it was just a venue for work; it was an opportunity for work, as it was for my mother too.[1]

Children of Italians born in London joined and attended Italian classes. Albert Cavalli was born on 1 January 1923 in London. His father, Casimiro, was a member of the *fascio* and sent Albert to the Italian day school:

Did it preach fascism? I don't recall it. You were too busy learning the cultural side of Italy ... I must point out that the advantage that we boys had of going to Italian school, not only to day school, but the evening classes, was that we would go to Italy every year, always to Cattolica, where there was a holiday resort and it was for the children of Italians abroad, not only from London, but from all over the place, and we used to go every year.

Didn't cost us anything, just the fare. As far as we were concerned those days under fascism for us were quite good ... we enjoyed ourselves under fascism, we didn't see any harm in it.[2]

Rita Pezzani was born in London in 1926. Her mother and father ran a café in Red Lion Street and sent Rita and her brothers to the Littorio:

> My mother used to go there one day a week and they used to do sewing and that for the poor, or they had the club there where my father would play cards. My brother was a 'Piccolo Balilla' and I was a 'Piccola Italiana' [the female version of the Balilla]. We used to go to all the sports grounds at Edgware and it was quite something. As far as politics ... I don't know ... I always thought that being a 'Piccola Italiana' was like being a girl guide – this is my opinion – or the boy scouts for the boys ... you know, this was the kind of thing ... there didn't seem to be anything wrong [with it].[3]

According to Graziella, most of the Italians who went to the Littorio were nominal members who wanted to take advantage of the cultural activities, be among other Italians in a safe environment and express patriotism rather than fascist ideology. For those who had been in Britain for many years, it was flattering that the government was showing an interest in their lives:

> I will say this, I don't believe that 90 per cent ... more than 90 per cent of the people involved, the Italians involved had a remote idea of what fascism was. They knew that Mussolini was a dictator, that he was the leader of Italy, there was a fascist regime, but they only saw the perks of the regime, the schools, the Casa del Littorio, lovely holidays and so on and so forth. I don't honestly think that they knew what fascism was. They just took the perks and didn't think very much about the lack of intellectual freedom and all the rest of the implications of fascism.[4]

Keen to spread the ideology, fascism used the successful model created in London to reach out to Italians in other parts of Britain. The second most important *fascio* or Casa d'Italia was founded in 1922 in Glasgow. By 1925 it was holding Italian classes and had a function similar to that of the London *fascio*. *Fasci* were then established in

Edinburgh, Manchester, Liverpool, Leeds, Sheffield, Cardiff, Aberdeen and Dundee.

Membership of the *fascio* was not compulsory, and many Italians were not members for various reasons. Most of the *fasci* in Britain were in city centres, and Italians living in coastal areas or in rural parts would have been unlikely to have the time to visit them. Many Italians were working class and had little opportunity for education, and their children were expected to go and work in the family business rather than pursue an education or even have time for a holiday. These children often spoke English and the dialect they learned from their parents, and never learned to speak Italian. Also, many Italians were apolitical; they had not taken an interest in politics and, more importantly for them, Italian politicians hadn't previously taken an interest in their lives. Often Italians were religious rather than political and used the churches to satisfy their social needs.

If fascism was born in Italy then so too was anti-fascism. There were Italians in Britain who were opposed to Mussolini's fascist government: Italians such as Decio Anzani. By 1940 he had lived in Britain for over 30 years and was a tailor with a workshop in Pollen Street, in London's Mayfair. He campaigned to raise awareness in Britain of the detrimental effects that fascism had on democracy, human rights and freedom of expression. In 1935 he had been involved in issuing pamphlets about Mussolini's imperial aims in Africa, called 'Mussolini, Abyssinia and War'. His teenage daughter Renée would help in the campaigning too.

Despite British opposition to Italy's invasion of Abyssinia and sanctions imposed on the country, the *fasci* were allowed to function as normal. Indeed, as a gesture of support, the London *fascio* met to salute the legions leaving Italy and began a collection of money, and of gold, for the cause. Other *fasci* around the country did the same, with Italian women exchanging their gold wedding rings for metal ones. In total around £19,480 was raised in this way from the Consuls of London, Glasgow, Dublin, Liverpool and Cardiff in 1936.

Although the relationship between the countries at this point was somewhat strained, Britain considered the fascist regime in Italy positively. Politicians including Churchill along with various newspaper owners had spoken openly in support of it. Fascism was preferable to communism, the natural enemy of British Imperialism. However, with the Second World War this viewpoint was changing dramatically, and associations with the party, once seemingly innocent and nominal, were coming to have very different connotations. Membership was regarded as sufficient grounds for suspicion, since it involved an oath of fidelity to its leader, Mussolini, and a promise to shed blood for the cause if necessary.

4

Fifth Columnists

Most of the 70,000 or so alien refugees who had searched for and been given sanctuary in Britain were from Germany and Austria. However, several hundred Italians had also left Italy prior to the war because of anti-Semitism. Unlike Nazism, fascism at its inception did not appear to be an anti-Semitic movement: there were Jews in the party, and a mistress of Mussolini was Jewish. However, by 1938 this had changed and the fascist government passed laws barring Italian Jews from performing certain jobs. Rather than being a change in ideology, it was a compromise with Italy's relationship with Hitler's Germany. One Italian Jew whom these laws impacted upon was Uberto Limentani, as his son Rupert explained:

> My father was born in 1913 and brought up in Milan, and it was a normal Italian family. He went to school in Milan and he went to university; he studied law at university in Milan and did the qualifying exams to become a practising barrister in the Milan law courts and he started

practising in the mid thirties. The Italian fascist government in power at the time introduced laws against the Jews, which meant that, apart from all the other things Jews were not allowed to do, he could no longer practise as a barrister, and his name was struck off the official list, the Albo of barristers, in the spring of 1939.[1]

Uberto made up his mind to leave Italy. After a certain amount of reflection he decided to go to Britain because he felt that he would be able to live more freely there, and he left Italy for the UK in June. By the time the war started he was working for the BBC in the Italian Broadcasting operation.

In the first few months of 1940 Italy had remained neutral, and therefore the British government had taken no action to intern members of the *fascio*, but soon the popular press began to take stock of Italians and journalists began to write articles about them. Using the words 'Italians' and 'fascism' together often made the two seem synonymous. On 27 April 1940, the *Daily Mirror* published an article about Italians in Britain:

There are more than twenty thousand Italians in Great Britain. London alone shelters more than eleven thousand of them. The London Italian is an indigestible unit of population. He settles here more or less temporarily, working until he has enough money to buy himself a little land in Calabria, or Campania or Tuscany. He often avoids employing British labour. It is much cheaper to bring a few relations into England from the old hometown. And so the boats unloaded all kinds of brown-eyed Francescas and Marias, beetle-browed Ginos, Titos and Marios ... now every Italian colony in Great Britain and America is a seething cauldron of smoking Italian politics. Black Fascism. Hot as Hell. Even the peaceful, law abiding proprietor of the back-street coffee shop bounces into a fine patriotic frenzy at the sound of Mussolini's name ... we are nicely honeycombed with little cells of potential betrayal. A storm is brewing in the Mediterranean. And we, in our droning, silly tolerance are helping it to gather force.[2]

In 1940 the *Daily Mirror* was selling around 1.4 million copies. It had positioned itself as the paper for the ordinary soldier and civilian and was a left-wing publication. The article was critical of the Italian use of chain migration, employing family as staff members, and the Italians' transient position in society, using Britain as a place to earn money to send back to Italy rather than making Britain their home. Articles written about Italians would have been read all over the country by British citizens and by the Italian residents that the articles were describing, the so-called Francescas, Marias, Ginos, Titos and Marios. Up until this point the British public were not swayed in a significant way against Italians in Britain and many British people would have read this article in an Italian temperance bar, confectionery shop or indeed back-street coffee shop. Although the situation in Europe was deteriorating rapidly, the xenophobic commentary by the popular press had little impact in stirring up hostility towards a community of people who were well known and, counter to what the article described, integrated rather than transient in their neighbourhoods.

By May 1940, the war was ten months old and the German army had successfully invaded Poland, Denmark, Norway, Luxembourg, Holland, Belgium and France. With the situation deteriorating by the day, Winston Churchill replaced Neville Chamberlain as British Prime Minister and

Minister for Defence. He addressed the House for the first time as Prime Minister on 13 May 1940, saying: 'I have nothing to offer but blood, toil, tears and sweat.'[3] The German front line had advanced with speed through blitzkrieg and Britain faced its greatest threat of invasion in over a thousand years. Twenty-one miles of water were all that separated Britain from the German forces, and fear of invasion led the popular press to run articles that called for the general internment of all enemy aliens, including those who had previously been given a tribunal under Chamberlain's government.

This fear had intensified in April 1940 following the German invasion of Norway, blame for which was directed at a fifth column – an army already within the country's defences. Its head was the leader of the Norwegian Nazi party, Vidkun Quisling, who in return for his collaboration was awarded dictatorial power in Norway by the Germans.

Churchill began to echo the popular press, calling for large roundups of enemy aliens including Germans and Austrians who had been given tribunals when Chamberlain was Prime Minister and classified as either 'A', 'B' or 'C'. Home Secretary John Anderson opposed Churchill because the security services had assured him that there was no evidence to suggest the existence of a fifth column in Britain. However, a new set of initiatives was taken, and on 12 May all male Germans and Austrians aged between 16 and 60 living in areas of possible military operations were interned. Initially the east and south coasts were targeted. Then on 17 May it was agreed that category 'B' aliens within the same age group and nationalities would be interned regardless of where they lived. By 27 May the Home Office had ordered the internment by police of Austrian and German category 'B' women aged 16 to 60.

On 29 May the War Cabinet discussed the possibility of Italian entry into the war. With the possibility of Mussolini's Italy joining the Axis powers, the subject of what to do with the Italians in Britain was back on the agenda. On 30 May plans were made to intern 1,500 Italians and 300 British subjects of Italian origin, a total higher than the previous figures of 1,200 and 300 respectively. At this stage not one of the people on these lists had been given a tribunal, and decisions were made in the absence of intelligence on individual circumstances.

5

'Bloody Italians'

On 10 June 1940, Italians resident in Britain finally received the news that they had feared the most. At 4.45 p.m., Benito Mussolini announced from the Palazzo Venezia in Rome that Italy had entered the Second World War on the side of Germany, and thus had declared war on Britain and France. 'It was on the radio,'[1] said Bruna Bonino, at the time a 14-year-old schoolgirl working in her father's café in Cock Lane, London. 'Italy had declared war on England,'[2] added Aurelio Tarquini, then a nine-year-old schoolboy from Elephant and Castle. 'I knew that there was something wrong because my parents were very upset,'[3] said Clementina Cordani from Wales, aged nine in 1940. In Glasgow, Joe Pieri was working behind the counter in the family fish and chip shop when he learned the news:

> Yes, well ... war broke and we learned about it –
> remember there were no televisions, there was the
> wireless ... the radio ... and it was well into the afternoon
> before I was told Italy had declared war. A policeman

39

friend of mine said, 'Look, Joe, we don't know what is going to happen – you better close the shop.'[4]

Italy's declaration of war was a surprise to Italians in Britain. The two countries had been allies in the First World War and many had assumed that they would be again. There was an immediate backlash by the public. Angry mobs directed their anger at Italian shops on the high streets of Britain. Joe Pieri followed the instruction of his policeman friend, closed the fish and chip shop for the night and went upstairs to the flat he lived in:

> By this time it was about six o' clock in the evening. And, about an hour after that, I could hear shouts in the street below and I looked out of the window and I could see a cart being pushed down Renfrew Street – that was where our shop was – and there were a crowd, I don't know possibly 50 to 60, possibly even more ... a hundred people ... and they were all shouting and swearing, 'bloody Italians, Italian bastards', and stopped in front of the shop and one of them shouted, 'That's a tally [slang for Italian] shop, do it in.' So they smashed the windows, they put bricks through the windows, they bashed the door open with an improvised battering ram – it was a

big tall wooden door – and they vandalised the shop completely, stripped all the fittings, broke them, took all the stock ... not that there was much stock to be taken – a few packets of cigarettes because it was a fish and chip shop and we didn't carry much stock. But the shop was ruined, the shop was smashed and I remember looking out of the window, I don't know what my feelings were, I was a bit numb, I was probably scared ... I probably was. And that was it. This went on for about 15 minutes, maybe even more, and then they piled all the stones back onto the pushcart and presumably went off to do another Italian shop in.[5]

Vandalism against Italian property erupted throughout the country. The large economic base of catering, with shops on the high street, meant that Italians were easy to find. Fosca Rendina, who had been born in London, was aged 15 at the time. Her family lived in Woodford but had a café in Upton Park, where she would help out after school and at weekends. Fosca remembered the day after Italy's declaration of war:

We woke ... we thought, what are we going to do now? We will just carry on as normal ... But then they started calling us horrible names and throwing stones at the windows, you know, and shouting and we thought, Oh my god what's happening ... What's happening to us, what are we going to do? So we thought, let's go up to the next floor ... but then they knew because if we wasn't downstairs we must be on the next floor up and we went up to the top floor and stones were coming in but we hid in the wardrobe until the next morning ... and then we went up to Woodford, and good job we had the house there.[6]

Within the backlash, some customers came to the aid of their local cafés. Fourteen-year-old Rita Pezzani experienced the xenophobes and the xenophiles in the same day at the family café in Poplar:

As they [mother and aunt] opened the shop they [vandals] were throwing stones at the windows and that. Tram drivers and conductors, they stood outside and they said, 'This family have served us for years, leave them alone, they are doing a good job,' and then of course my mother was able to carry on working.[7]

To avoid being the focus of the anti-Italian sentiment, shops began to display signs declaring that they had sons in the British army.

Under the Aliens Act, employed Italians faced a dramatic change in their circumstances too. Aurelio Tarquini's father worked as a chef in a restaurant in the West End of London:

> I wasn't working at the time, I was too young [eight years old] but my father was working with my eldest brother and they were kicked out of their job immediately that night. My father had the day off and my brother was told to tell my father not to come back anymore, and he never worked again for six and a half years because they weren't allowed to employ alien Germans or Italians.[8]

Italians living in areas of possible military operations near the coast were dealt another blow and faced eviction from their homes. A letter was sent to aliens informing them as follows:

> No foreigner can enter into, or reside in, any area declared to be a Protected Area without the written

permission of the Chief Constable. Notice is hereby given to you that you, being an alien and being resident in an area declared to be a Protected Area, are required to take immediate steps to remove from this area, and that if you are found in this area after the expiry of three days from the date of this notice, steps will be taken to enforce the Order against you.[9]

Most Italians who lived in restricted areas by the coast were ice cream or fish and chip shop proprietors and were unable to gain exemption. It was common for Italians to live above their own shops, and the Order effectively made them simultaneously unemployed and homeless. For many, accommodation would be sought with family and friends, as three days was too short a time to make permanent arrangements, and given the prevailing hostility to aliens it was virtually impossible to find landlords willing to accommodate them. However, it was the decision taken by the British Prime Minister that would have the biggest impact.

Upon hearing the Italian declaration of war on Britain, Churchill ordered the immediate bombing of munitions factories in Milan. On the home front, he issued the instruction for the security service and the police to carry out a general internment of Italian men in Britain. Displaying no regard for the arrangements made prior to 10 June, *every* Italian male in Britain was to be arrested and interned regardless of whether or not they were members of the *fascio*.

6

Internment

On 11 June, at 6.30 a.m., two plain-clothes policemen knocked on the door of Ettore and Tina Feraboli in Clapham. One of the detectives said: 'Mr Feraboli, will you please get together a few things in a suitcase because unfortunately we have to detain you for a short while.'[1] Ettore did as he was asked, and left with the police. Tina contacted the school in Portsmouth where their daughter Graziella had been evacuated, and asked to have her sent back to London. Graziella remembered:

> My mother called the school and said to the headmistress, 'Reverend Mother Superior send my daughter home immediately.' And within the day, the Reverend Mother had called me in and said, 'Italy has joined the war.' I can remember stupidly looking up at her and saying, 'Surely on the side of the Allies,' and she just looked at me with a funny sort of smile and she said, 'No, I'm sorry.' And so she packed me onto a coach and I arrived at Victoria station where my mother met me and

the first thing she said as I got off the coach was, 'Your father's gone, they've taken him away.'[2]

In the days after Italy's declaration of war, thousands of arrests were carried out. In back rooms and upstairs apartments, Italians who had just witnessed the destruction of their shops frantically phoned the police for assistance; but rather than coming to aid them, the police often had a very different objective when they arrived.

In Glasgow, Joe Pieri had barricaded himself in the flat above his recently vandalised fish and chip shop. The arrival of the police came as no surprise to him. A policeman friend of his had forewarned him that he faced arrest and he was expecting them:

At about three o' clock in the morning a knock came at the door and there were two policeman who invited me to go along with them, and there waiting at the bottom of the steps was a Black Maria – that was the name given to the police vans of those days, they were painted black with a little grille at the back – and they loaded me onto that and there were already four Italians that had been

picked up before me and the five of us were taken to
Maitland Street police station.[3]

Fellow Glaswegian Rando Bertoia was also on the
police's list. Rando was born in June 1920 in Montereale
Valcellina, in the province of Pordenone in the Friuli-
Venezia Giulia region of Italy. At the age of five he and his
mother and father moved to Glasgow, where his father then
worked for Toffolo Jackson, a large *terrazzo* (mosaic) firm.
The police arrested Rando and his father the day after
Italy's declaration of war:

> Yes ... aye ... so the policemen came to the door on June
> the 11th 1940 and took my father and myself to the
> police station. They were 'very sorry', they said: 'It's our
> job but you won't be very long there, only a couple of
> days.' So we went there to the police station and there
> was a lot of Italians there, some born here, some came
> from Italy and had ice cream shops, and so on. So I knew
> one or two but not very many because I was not in that
> game.[4]

Many of the arrests were carried out at their homes in the early hours, when men were either preparing to go or had already left for work, so housewives and children opened the front door and were met by police. Maria Moruzzi was a recent arrival in Britain from Bardi, a province of Parma, Emilia-Romagna. She was 18 and had been married to her husband John for around a year when he was arrested in London:

> Two plain-clothes policemen knocked on the door and said, 'We are policemen,' and then said, 'We have come to take your husband with us.' 'Uh,' I said, 'but my husband is at work.' 'Yes, we know he is at work, but we want to tell you to prepare a suitcase for him because we are taking him with us.' 'But what has happened to my husband, what has happened to my John?' I was very scared.[5]

In most cases the arrests were carried out in front of frightened children. In Wales, six-year-old Clementina Cordani witnessed the arrest of her father:

They knocked on the door, six great big policemen came in, well they were big to me, I was only six, and they said, 'We're going to take you away,' to my father. He said, 'How can I leave my wife and little girl, I mean you can see the state my wife is in [pregnant].' 'No, no, you got to go.' So they took Dad, and I can remember – as I say, it's a long time ago, but I can remember distinctly – they had hold of my father's arms taking him out, and these were handcuffed. And when I think of it now, why did they handcuff him but ... there you are, I suppose people tried to get away, I don't know, but that was a thing that's been in my mind ever since, it was terrible.[6]

Local policemen had been given the embarrassing job of arresting respectable members of the community whom they had known for many years, and some policemen were willing to look the other way. Bruna Bonino was 14 years old when two policemen from Snow Hill police station came knocking at the door of the family café in Cock Lane near Smithfield Market in London:

They were very good, the police, because they knew my father, they called him Peter, knew us all ... one of the policemen turned round and said, 'Make a run for it.' My dad said, 'Where do you think I'm going to run to? You might as well take me, you know. I've got to go, you might as well, let's go.'[7]

Although Aurelio Tarquini's father had lost his job because he had become an enemy alien, he escaped the blanket internment:

> My father had a strong accent, spoke English well but he had a strong accent, and when he went to give his address at the police station where he had to register he said, 'I live in number 48 Peckham Road,' but it sounded like Packman Road, and when we moved from Peckham Road to Forest Hill, we had to get permission to move. He went to the police station and they said to him, 'Where have you been? We've been looking all over for you, where do you live?' '48 Peckham Road.' 'Peckham Road?' they said. 'Yeah.' 'Oh, we've been looking for Packman Road.' They couldn't find him and he was under their noses all the time.[8]

After being arrested, the men were taken to their local police station. 'We were put in a cell,' said Joe Pieri, who found himself in the company of other Scottish Italians:

> We were fairly treated and the thing was that I knew practically every policeman in that police station because they had been regular customers of mine in the shop.[9]

As well as issuing orders to arrest every Italian-born man, the authorities had instructed the police and security services to arrest some 600 British-born Italians, double the initial 300. As it was against the law to arrest British citizens without charge, the government used Defence Regulation 18B, which gave them the power to detain.

Albert Cavalli was 17 years of age when he was detained by the police under the regulation and was sent to HM Prison Brixton in South London:

> Well you go in, they strip-search [you], have a bath, just in case you got some disease or something like that, and then they take you to the cell, you know, and lock you in until the next morning. I remember when I woke up I didn't want to open my eyes, I thought I'm dreaming, I can't be where I think I am. I opened my eyes slowly and I

saw these three bloody walls and this big iron door in front of me. And I heard the clanging of doors being opened, application to the governor, slops out and all that.[10]

In Brixton Prison, Albert was imprisoned in cell number 35. In cell number 34 was Oswald Mosley, the leader of the British Union of Fascists, and directly opposite Admiral Sir Barry Domvile, President of the Anglo-German Link, along with his son. These British citizens were also interned under Defence Regulation 18B. Several months later Albert was given a tribunal:

I went to the tribunal and I had Sir Roland Campbell there and two other bods and the usual questions, 'What are your leanings, are you Italian or British?' I was a bit wittier in those days, well you've made up your mind what I am, that's why I'm here. 'What would you be prepared to do if we released you?' I said first of all you release my father, then I will think about it. 'You can't tell us what to do!' No, that's it, I said. You've interned my father, he's been here since 1920, and he's never been back to Italy. He's been a good citizen, paid his taxes and everything else, and yet you've interned him. All he wanted to do was work and make a living for himself and us children. 'That's all right, you can go,' and that's all I heard.[11]

Following his tribunal Albert was not released from Brixton Prison. He remained there for six months and spent 23 hours a day in his cell, one of 600 British-born Italians languishing in prisons around Britain under Defence Regulation 18B. In addition, in the days following Italy's declaration of war some 4,100 Italian nationals were interned in transit camps across the country.

7

Wharf Mills

After being taken to local police stations and held for a few days, Italian men were taken to alien collecting stations. These were usually army barracks or camps on racecourses. The main alien collecting stations for Italians were at Edinburgh in Scotland, Kempton Park in Surrey, Lingfield in Surrey, Paignton in Devon, Pembroke in Wales and Southampton in Hampshire.

Fences with barbed wire entanglements surrounded the camps and armed guards patrolled the perimeters. The hasty measures of internment were reflected in the hastily improvised camps, and rather than being quartered in purpose-built structures, men slept on palliasses inside horseboxes.

The National Service Act (1939) and blanket internment sometimes reunited families in the most extraordinary ways, with internees finding themselves being guarded by their *own* sons.

In Wales, Dino Viazzani, aged 19 at the time, had
been arrested, along with his elderly father, by local police.
After a night in the police cell followed by a transfer to
Brecon Barracks, they were in Cardiff waiting to be
transported to a location undisclosed to them:

> There was a man from Grezzo, a village near here [hamlet
> of Bardi]. His name was Albertelli. His son was outside
> the train guarding his father with a gun with a bayonet.
> He said to the sergeant, 'Can I go and speak to my son?'
> 'No, you can't speak to your son, your son is your enemy,'
> he said. 'What, my son, my enemy?' 'Yes, your son is your
> enemy because he was born in England and you're an
> Italian.' What a stupid thing to say to an old man, your
> son is your enemy.[1]

One of the largest camps was in Bury, to the North of
England. After three weeks, Graziella and Tina Feraboli
received a letter from Ettore, from an address near
Manchester. This was the first piece of news they'd had
from him since his arrest on 10 June:

We discovered he was detained in a camp in the north of
England; Wharf Mills was the name of the camp. He had
managed to send a letter, censored of course, on special
paper that was given to them to write on, and then it said,
'Opened by the censor.' In his broken English he wrote
that he was obviously terribly concerned about us, he had
no news, he knew nothing of what was happening to us.[2]

Ettore, along with thousands of other Italian men,
had been sent to a transit camp in a disused nineteenth-
century cotton mill in Bury, Lancashire. On Wednesday, 12
June 1940, the first Italian enemy aliens began to arrive
there. Given that Italy had only declared war on Britain and
France two days earlier, these would most certainly have
come from Manchester's 'Little Italy' community in Ancoats.

According to the *Bury Times* published on Saturday,
15 June, 'The Italians began to arrive on the 12th and by the
evening of the Wednesday around five hundred Italians had
entered the camp. As the Italians entered, some 1,200
German aliens were moved out.'[3] (By the time Italy entered
the war, the War Cabinet had initiated a policy of general
internment for all male Germans and Austrians, subject to
exemptions in certain categories. Female Germans and

Austrians in category 'B' between the ages of 16 and 60 were also interned.) The *Bury Times* went on to describe the arrival of the Italians as follows:

> As the Germans left by train, the newly interned Italians arrived by police car, Manchester Corporation double decker buses and trains. Upon arrival, each Italian was medically examined and asked to give his particulars before being shown to his quarters. The quarters were in the confines of the factory surrounded by barbed wire entanglements and heavily guarded by armed soldiers. Quarters were either on one of the three floors of the factory, or in the tents, which had been erected in the adjoining fields. Whereas the Germans had ranged in age from youths to elderly men, most of the Italians who had arrived by Wednesday were of middle age or over. Nearly all of them had their belongings in attaché cases or suitcases. About half of the Italians in the camp on Wednesday were working class men. The Italians had hoped against hope that their country would remain non-belligerent, and every one of them had a sad look as he was taken into the camp. For the first day at least there were none of the fancy dishes for which the Italians are famous. The aliens helped to prepare and serve good,

wholesome stew. They could help themselves to as much as they wished from the dixie (a large metal pot for cooking) brought around the dining quarters. New sanitary arrangements – as good as those provided for the soldiers – have been substituted for those formerly used by the cotton operatives.[4]

None of the 'fancy dishes' that the Italians were famous for were available, but some of the Italian chefs and restaurant managers from London's West End were at Wharf Mills: Cesare Bianchi, head chef at the Café Royal; Italo Zangiacomi (61), general manager of the Piccadilly Hotel; Cesare Borgo, manager of the Café Anglais; Hector (Ettore) Zavattoni (58), banqueting manager of the Savoy Hotel and Luigi Vergano, late chef at Quaglino.

The *Bury Times* article concluded: 'Up to two thousand aliens can be accommodated in the three storeys of the mill.'[5] However, as June progressed the numbers arriving surpassed the numbers leaving, and the facility rapidly reached and exceeded its capacity. By the time Joe Pieri, along with many other Scottish Italians, had arrived from Glasgow, the camp was very different from the one described in the *Bury Times*. According to Joe: 'Wharf Mills in Bury near Liverpool, that was a bit of a hell hole ... it was like something out of Dickens, broken glass, dust in the air from the old mills that had been there and broken machinery.'6 The planned sanitary arrangements could not cope with the vast numbers that were quartered there. Joe said:

> There were about 40 water taps for all the people that were there, about five thousand people. You had to queue up for water, queue up to wash. The latrines were absolutely choked; you just did your needs in a corner. It wasn't pretty.7

Dino Viazzani had arrived from Wales at Wharf Mills transit camp, along with his elderly father. They tried to improve the conditions in which they found themselves: 'You can imagine ... the floor was covered in grease, but within a few days with wheelbarrows and whatever, we cleaned up the place.'8

The War Office was responsible for the camp, but with the responsibility of organising the withdrawal from Dunkirk, re-equipping the British Expeditionary Force and recruiting fresh age groups to meet a threat of invasion, internment was probably given less attention and less manpower with little understanding of the task at hand. However draconian and vermin-infested the conditions were at Wharf Mills, internees had the opportunity to write home. Their relatives, among them Graziella, were relieved and overjoyed to hear from them:

> He wrote a very short note, but being my father and always being very serene ... and not wanting to worry my mother, he said he was fine, he was with a lot of other Italians, and there was nothing to worry about but he was very worried about us, could we please send him news immediately. Well, I think my mother must have done [so] but I don't think he got it because shortly afterwards our neighbours received a letter. My father wrote to our neighbours saying, 'I have no news of my family, would you please keep an eye on them and eventually let me know if they are alright?'[9]

Letters and parcels could take from five days to five weeks to arrive, and as the camps were transit camps, letters and parcels rarely made it to the intended recipient or might be emptied of their contents along the way.

Some families members were in no doubt as to what had happened to their interned fathers after their arrest because they had been interned along with them: from Glasgow, Rando Bertoia and his father; and from Wales, Dino Viazzani and his father. The brothers Angelo and Santo Albericci, who worked at the Queen's Hotel in Leeds and the Midland Hotel in Manchester, respectively, were interned together along with their brother-in-law, Peter Anselmi. These small groups of men later organised themselves by national groups – 'Scottish', 'English' and 'Welsh'. Separated from their families, unsure what lay ahead, they waited for the British authorities to decide their fate.

8

The Lists

As the Germans advanced and the Low Countries fell within days of being attacked, the Aliens Act, which had already been used to intern enemy aliens, was used again. The Act allowed the government not only to intern aliens but also to deport them if the security services perceived them to be a threat to the security of Britain. The British government was, by law, not allowed to deport British nationals.

By 24 May 1940 Churchill was advocating a policy of deporting all internees and prisoners of war out of Britain, with the priority given to prisoners of war, interned seamen and category 'A' enemy aliens. The matter of deportation was handed over to the Lord President of the Council, the former British Prime Minister Neville Chamberlain, and within meetings the possibility of aliens being received by the dominions and colonies overseas was discussed.

On 3 June Lord Swinton, on behalf of the Home Defence Security Executive (which had been formed on 10

May 1940 under General Sir Edmund Ironside, Commander-in-Chief Home Forces, to organise the defence of Britain from invasion by the Axis powers), proposed to the Lord President that as many internees and prisoners of war as possible should be transferred, including category 'A' Germans and prisoners of war and category 'A' Italians. It was proposed that as many as 9,500 Italians should be transferred, with different orders of priority. The 1,500 category 'A' Italian aliens on the list of *fascio* members made by MI5 would be deported first. The policy of interning the men had changed to a policy of deporting them instead.

On 11 June, the day after Italy's declaration of war, the War Cabinet discussed deportation and it was explained that persons on the Italian embassy list were to be allowed to proceed to Italy on a special ship, and a corresponding shipload of British subjects would be allowed to leave Italy. The Italian Ambassador, Giuseppe Bastianini, nominated 730 Italians to be repatriated. As Churchill had ordered the internment of all Italian men in Britain, many of those on the list were in police cells and alien collecting stations. For Italian families who accepted the Ambassador's offer, it meant a journey to Glasgow docks to board a ship called the *Monarch of Bermuda*, which carried 629 Italians including men, women and children, led by Ambassador Bastianini. The ship sailed to Lisbon, where it docked on 26 June, and the passengers were transferred directly to the *Conte Rosso*, which had arrived from Italy with the British Embassy staff, in exchange for a reciprocal number of expatriate British citizens. The *Monarch of Bermuda* subsequently sailed back to Britain and the *Conte Rosso* to Italy. A few Italians who had been on the Ambassador's list rejected the offer of repatriation, including Rita Pezzani's father:

> The Ambassador phoned to say that Italy had come into the war and there was a ship going back to Italy ... it would take my father ... and also the rest of the family. But my father, because he was the eldest son ... and [because] his father was here ... said, 'Well, if we go, what will happen to our property? We'd better stay here to look after our property.' The younger brother was married to an English lady but [had] no children and he didn't want to go back. So the other two brothers and brother-in-law and their families, they went back, they were on the boat [*Monarch of Bermuda*], they went to

Glasgow, from Glasgow to Lisbon and they spent the war in Italy.[1]

At the War Cabinet meeting on 11 June it was also suggested that the right course would be to keep 1,500 desperadoes (*fascio* Italians) in this country and to deport as many of the others as possible to Italy. The policy underlying this decision was that many of the Italians who were being exchanged were unwilling to leave Britain and would form centres of disaffection in Italy. These considerations did not apply to the 1,500 desperadoes, who, if returned to Italy, were perceived to have a possible value to the Italian war effort. It seems, however, that transport difficulties led to this scheme being abandoned, and all category 'A' Italians were consequently among those for early shipment to one of the dominions.

On Monday, 17 June, a conference was held at the War Office to discuss the movement of prisoners of war and internees to Canada. Among those present were officials from the Home Office, Canada House, the Dominions Office, the Foreign Office and MI5. The representative from Canada House, Mr Ritchie, stated that Canada was prepared to take 7,000 prisoners of war and internees. The Foreign Office, represented by Mr Farquar, stated that they had no objection to Italians being sent to Canada. It was agreed that the total of 7,000 should be made up of 2,600 category 'A' Germans and Austrians, 1,900 prisoners of war and 1,500 *fascio* Italians. These numbers did not include the repatriated Italians who left for Italy in exchange for British diplomats. Within the group of Germans and Austrians were men who had been given a tribunal upon entering Britain when Neville Chamberlain was Prime Minister. However, several hundred who had been given a category 'B' or 'C' were re-categorised as 'A' to be deported. Among the names was that of Conrad Lamberty, who was born in Aachen, in Germany. He was 74 years old. There were also 123 German merchant seamen who had automatically been given category 'A' status when captured at sea.

With the addition of 700 military guards, this would make a total of 6,700 men, leaving a margin of 300 for emergencies. The military guards were made up of several regiments and battalions and included the 9th Battalion, Cameronians (Scottish Rifles), where Peter Tarchetti was serving as a rifleman. Four ships were available to transport internees, including the *Duchess of York*, the

Ettrick and the *Arandora Star*. The port of embarkation would be Glasgow or Liverpool. The first ship to leave with internees aboard was the *Duchess of York*, with 2,000 category 'A' Germans and Austrians and 535 prisoners of war, on the 21 June.

On the same day a list of names for deportation on subsequent ships was sent to camps around the country where Italians were being held. When the Prisoners of War Directorate were making up the party for deportation they collected 717 Italians from the various camps up and down the country who were believed to be on the list of category 'A' Italians. Over half the number on the list were unaccounted for. Some of the names that appeared had left the country or had not been interned. The camp commandants had 24 hours to identify those to be deported. The work was carried out under great pressure, and some of the names on the list had alternative spellings, which led to ambiguity in selecting the correct person. At this stage the War Cabinet endorsed the policy that the only categories to be exempted from deportation were men required for war production; men interned in error; and men with wives and children in Britain. Therefore young single Italian men were also included in the categories of those to be deported. Included among them was Joe Pieri:

> My name was called out together with four hundred and three other Italians. We were mixed in with a bunch of Germans. Most of them as I remember were Jewish refugees but there was one contingent of about seven hundred soldiers, Marines and Luftwaffe men who had been shot down over France and Marines that had been captured at the Narvik landings in Norway.[2]

When the lists arrived at Wharf Mills and the roll calls were announced, the natural groups that had formed among the men were divided. Fathers and sons found themselves separated. Rando Bertoia and his father were two such internees. Rando's name was on a list of men who faced deportation (likely to be the list of young, single Italian men) and his father was on a list of those to be taken to the Isle of Man (Italian, not a member of the *fascio* and married).

> They just started calling people's names. Some of them were about 70 or 80. I was one of the youngest, and well,

I felt sorry for them. I was young so I didn't mind so much and my father remained there and of course I said, 'Cheerio', and my father said to a friend, 'Look after my boy,' and he said, 'Aye, I'll look after him,' and that was it.[3]

Ettore Giannotti and his father Alfredo were in the same group as Rando, along with the brothers Angelo and Santo Albericci, but their brother-in-law Peter Anselmi was called to a different group. Some of the men could not comprehend being separated from family members and changed groups in order to remain with their relatives. It is therefore likely that men not on lists for deportation ended up in groups to be deported. The categorisation of the men depended on the lists prepared by MI5, but the security service, beyond indicating the categories of enemy aliens who in their opinion should be despatched first, had nothing to do with the actual arrangements for their departure. No lists were ever submitted to the security service for checking.

At this stage, Joe, Rando and Ettore had no idea that they were being deported to Canada because they were labelled category 'A'. They had been given no tribunal and no information. Those whose names were not on the list of category 'A' Italians were to be sent to the Isle of Man instead. They numbered around 3,000 Italian 'enemy aliens' and 600 British-born Italians.

9

The Isle of Man

The Isle of Man had been used for the internment of German nationals in the First World War and was used again in the Second, but on a much larger scale. There were six camps for Germans and Austrians, three for Italians, two for women, and one for British citizens interned under Defence Regulation 18B. Dino Viazzani and his father were both sent to the Isle of Man. After a short and terrifying trip, in the middle of the night in pitch dark on an overloaded ferry, they landed at a port on the Island and were escorted to their camp. They were met by locals hostile to their arrival:

> When we got there, the people in the streets ... they were all waiting for [us] and they were spitting on us, throwing things at us, everything, anything they could find and they kept saying, 'Mussolini, Mussolini.' Some of us said, 'It's not our fault if Mussolini declared war against your country; it's just one of them things.' We went on and on, [and] then we came to our camp, Palace Camp, which was

a cage. They opened all these big gates and we just walked in and everyone had to find your own place your own room and everything.[1]

The camps were rows of terraced boarding houses and small hotels lining the shore in Douglas, Ramsey and smaller seaside towns on the Island. They had been requisitioned and cleared of their usual summer visitors, surrounded by double coils of barbed wire, armed with sentries and given over to the British government to intern enemy aliens.

Seventeen-year-old Albert Cavalli and his father Casimiro were both interned on the Isle of Man but in different camps. Albert arrived later than his father, after having first spent six months in Brixton Prison and then time in a number of transit camps including Ascot (the winter quarters for the Bertram Mills Circus), York (a converted racecourse) and Huyton in Liverpool (a new estate surrounded by barbed wire), and was finally transferred to the Isle of Man in December 1941. He was initially sent to the camp holding British-born internees at Peel but was later transferred:

After a while, after a lot of negotiating and things like that, those of us with dual nationality, Italian nationality, could go and join our fathers or relatives in the Italian camp. I put my name down and within no time I was with my father ... and that was 1942 that I joined him, so for the first two years all the news that I got from my father were letters, nothing else, I never saw him.[2]

Upon arrival, life as an internee began. A house supervisor was elected and then above him a street supervisor and above him a camp supervisor or commandant. Internees were chosen to be in charge of the canteen, and it wasn't difficult to find volunteers, as most of the men had worked in the catering industry up until their arrests. Educational activities were organised among the men, including language classes. An interned Italian priest, who was a street supervisor, gave Albert the job of teaching Italian:

> It was surprising the amount of boys there who could not speak a word of Italian, that were born in Italy and had come over to this country when they were babies and

had never been back ... they didn't know any Italian at all, so I would teach them.[3]

From August 1940, both voluntary and paid work outside the camps was permitted. Although many Italians lived in urban areas of Britain, and predominantly worked in the catering industry, many of the men had come from rural backgrounds, had a good knowledge of agricultural work and went to work for the Isle of Man Agricultural Board: 'They used to hire them out to these farmers,' said Vito Maestranzi, whose father was interned for four years. 'He used to get one shilling a day. They used to take them with a soldier; you know, stay with them all day and take them back.'[4]

Initially, work parties and individuals were accompanied by an armed guard, but when it became evident that the men were harmless, the responsibility was given to the farmer rather than a guard, and a more relaxed and informal approach was adopted. Dino Viazzani had been in Britain a little under a year when he was interned at Palace Camp. He went to work for the Agricultural Board, which involved ploughing, and digging potatoes, sprouts, cabbages and leeks, and was also paid one shilling a day. At

the outset, an armed guard accompanied him but after
gaining the trust of the camp commandant, Lieutenant
Lipton, Dino was able to go with the farmer alone:

> I went with him. He introduced me to his family, which he
> wasn't supposed to do; I met his wife, I met his sons and
> daughters, and as soon as I got into the house he said to
> me, 'We don't want you to think that you are an internee
> and that you are an enemy of us. I don't want you to think
> that. You are welcome into our house like one of us.' I
> said, 'Thank you very much.' They gave me food, they
> really welcomed me … I wasn't an enemy to them, just an
> ordinary person like they were.[5]

The leisure facilities used by the holidaymakers in
peacetime were soon utilised by the authorities to stem the
boredom that existed in the camps. Albert Cavalli made the
most of the sea bathing, country walks and cinema visits
that were allowed under escort:

> I got to be fair, we weren't ill-treated, I mean especially in
> the Italian camps, they used to take us out for walks, with
> an unarmed escort, no rifle, no nothing … and they used
> to divide us into three groups, fast walkers, medium

walkers, slow walkers; we used to go out walking ... we used to go to the cinema, once a week, closed to the public ... we used to go in and it cost a shilling in those days, to go in.[6]

Eventually, the internees were allowed to send and receive letters. After seeing her father arrested, handcuffed and taken away, Clementina Cordani received a letter:

We didn't hear anything for ages and then I can remember, I had a letter from my father, he had somebody to write it in English ... he was saying, 'I hope you were a good girl,' and he mentioned a place [where he was] but they rubbed that out. Any mention of any places was rubbed out because they were all censored, you see.[7]

As well as letters, it was possible for internees to receive visitors on the Isle of Man. Many Italian women were aliens and therefore subject to restrictions on their movements, so it was left to their British-born children to make the visit instead. Fourteen-year-old Bruna Bonino lived in London with her mother and grandmother while her father was interned in the Isle of Man and her uncle had been deported. Bruna visited her father on the Isle of Man, accompanied by her cousin:

> I went twice to see my dad, and when I got there [I saw] all barbed wire, all the way round. Went in a great big room and just sat down, long table, I was one end, Dad was the other and two officers were walking round ... and [I] just asked, 'How you are?' And I think ... most of the time, I think I was crying. Can't remember what we said. We stayed at the Isle of Man in a bed and breakfast.[8]

Many of the men who lived in major cities such as London found themselves in relative safety in the internment camps on the Isle of Man. In September 1940, a few months into their internment, the bombers that the government had expected at the outbreak of the war in 1939 began to arrive over British cities. This caused them great concern because their families faced a significant threat. A blackout had been imposed at the start of the war and the daily ritual of drawing curtains, pulling down blinds and pinning blankets up could take hours, especially for houses with many windows. No light was allowed to be visible from flats, houses, offices, factories or shops. Those that didn't comply faced penalties. In 1940, some 300,000 people were taken to court for blackout offences. Bruna's mother was one of the thousands summoned to court:

> We had a letter to say we had to go to court and we wondered what happened, we didn't realise … you know … it was afterwards that we realised that Nonna [Grandmother], she'd forgot to pull the curtains for the blackout. When we went in front of the Judge he said, 'You've been signalling to the enemy.' I mean, we knew nothing about the enemy, you know, we were all innocent there … I mean, what can you say? 'Well I'm afraid that will be ten pounds'… I mean then, ten pounds was a lot of money. I think it was all the money Mum had.[9]

Across London, air raid precautions meant that people had to take cover in the Underground, or use air raid shelters; some people had shelters in their back garden and some were communal. Aurelio Tarquini was eight years old when he went to a communal air raid shelter with both his parents, as his father had not been interned on account of his name being spelled incorrectly on the police register. In these crowded, stressful environments sometimes abuse was thrown:

> We were insulted right, left and centre in the street. We were spat at, we were ill-treated … they tried to make it [so] that we could not use the surface shelter that was across the road that we were entitled to use because we were resident there and they tried to stop us going in there. They couldn't do that, so we used to go in there every night and lay down our mattress and sleep in the shelter, and on some nights they used to leave me because I was the youngest to stay there and keep the place, and at times that I was there, I was insulted.[10]

Alfred Tisi was 11 years old and living in London. He received letters from his anxious father on the Isle of Man:

> He must have been worried about us being under the Blitz, because for that time we lived in the air raid shelter because of the bombing. We were very lucky we were never bombed, but two or three doors away were, so just as well we were in the air raid shelter at that time.[11]

As well as farming, work of military importance in munitions factories in Britain was offered to internees, but many declined this type of work. Vito Maestranzi was born in London in 1931. When the war erupted he was left in Italy with his grandparents, but his father returned to London to work as a knife grinder and was interned. He was offered release on condition that he helped the British war effort:

> They offered Dad work in the government factories. He said, 'Well, if I have to work for the government it must be for munitions or planes or something. I've got my family in Italy,' he says, 'why should I go and work for something that might be used to kill my family in Italy?' So he said, 'No, I prefer to go and work in the fields; stay here and work in the fields rather than going out and working in a factory.'[12]

This was the case for many internees who were sympathetic to the British war effort but were reluctant to work in factories that produced arms that could be used against their relatives in Italy.

Although some declined the offer to help the British war effort in the factories, it was evident that many of the men were harmless so the Home Office appointed Sir Percy Lorraine, an ex-British Ambassador to Rome, to assess and classify the Italians and to initiate releases. By the end of November 1940, 410 internees had been released including Dino Viazzani's father: 'They didn't even understand why they'd picked him up,' said Dino; 'he was 64 years old then when the war broke out, and he wasn't in very good health.'[13]

Friends and relatives of internees wrote to the Home Office requesting early releases. In Tonypandy, in Wales, retired Major Richards took it upon himself to start a petition within the village vouching for the character and asking for the release of Clementina Cordanis's father Ernie:

He said, 'I've known Ernie since he was a boy, I will vouch for him.' He had everyone, the butcher, the milkman, the draper, the grocer, the priest, the doctor and Mrs Rogers, my neighbour, to sign the petition. They all knew Dad as Ernie and everyone gave their signature, you see. And then they said [to him], 'We are going to send you home for a month on trial and if you are all right after a month you will be reviewed but if not, you will be sent back straight away.' So he was here a month and then he was reviewed and they did that all the time.[14]

Ernie remained at home, subject to alien restrictions but close to his family and his newly born son.

Apart from those released early on, the Isle of Man would be home to thousands of Italians for the next four to five years. The internment of enemy aliens stopped on 15 July 1940. However, in October 1940 a group of around 42 Italians arrived on the Isle of Man for internment at Metropole Camp. They should have been in Canada. With their arrival came news of a terrible tragedy.

10

Arandora Star

In late June 1940, after being transferred from Wharf Mills, Joe Pieri, along with another 1,000 or so Italians and several hundred German and Austrian Jewish refugees and prisoners of war, found themselves at Liverpool Docks: 'There on the docks were two huge ships; the one that was moored directly beside us [the *Ettrick*] was bigger than the second one, which was moored slightly behind ... I could see the name, *Arandora Star*.'[1]

In the 1930s the *Arandora Star* was one of the most famous cruise liners in Europe, carrying passengers in the height of luxury to destinations such as Norway, the Mediterranean and the West Indies. She was much loved by those who travelled on her, and affectionately called the 'Wedding Cake', due to her white exterior and blue bunting. When war broke out in September 1939, the *Arandora Star* was ordered back to port by the Admiralty while on one of her pleasure cruises to the Norwegian fjords.

From the few references to the *Arandora Star* in

documents held by the Ministry of Defence, it would appear that in December 1939 she was taken up by the Admiralty for Net Defence development trials in Portsmouth. These involved the ship being fitted with anti-torpedo nets to her port and starboard sides and having dummy torpedoes fired upon her. These trials proved unsuccessful, and tests were abandoned. By June 1940 the *Arandora Star* was being used by the Ministry of War, on behalf of the Home Office, as a transport ship to carry internees across the Atlantic to camps in Canada.

In command of the *Arandora Star* was Captain Moulton. He was in his early fifties, had been captain of the ship in her days as a luxury liner and was still in command when she was a Ministry of War transport ship. His crew included Chief Officer F. Brown and Chief Engineer R. C. Connell. The Ministry of War had carried out a number of changes to the *Arandora Star*'s appearance. The ship had been painted grey, as were all ships that made the trans-Atlantic crossing. Her portholes were covered to stop light escaping and giving away the ship's position. As her cargo were enemy aliens, barbed wire had been placed on the decks and around lifeboats to protect areas that were vulnerable to escape. To secure the internees, the War Office provided a military guard led by Officer Commanding Major C. A. Bethell, Tank Corps. Other officers included Major G. A. I. Dury (Liaison Officer), Captain F. J. Robertson (Interpreter), Captain C. M. C. Lee (Interpreter) and Lieutenant J. F. Constable.

Joe wasn't to know that the *Arandora Star* was a former luxury cruise liner. She was camouflaged and armed: 'I remember distinctly a cannon on the back,' said Joe, 'and there were what seemed to me coils of barbed wire on the decks.'[2] Dino Viazzani remembered seeing the ship docked at Fleetwood, in Lancashire: 'When we saw this boat, the *Arandora Star*, black barbed wire everywhere, we could see the soldiers walking up and down.'[3]

However, one of the internees at Liverpool *did* recognise the ship from her days as a cruise liner. After leaving Italy for London in 1938 because of anti-Semitic laws, Uberto Limentani found work with the BBC in their Italian broadcasting operation. The job required him to pass a number of security checks and therefore it was assumed that he would avoid internment. Much to his surprise, he was now being deported on a ship that he had seen many years earlier, as his son Rupert explained:

> He had seen it moored in Venice opposite St Mark's Square, by the Giardini Publici [public gardens], and he recalled having thought at the time how nice it would be to have a cruise in a luxury ship like that, but in those circumstances at Liverpool the prospect seemed a lot less appealing.[4]

As a luxury liner, the *Arandora Star* had carried 354 first-class passengers and a crew of around 200. Twelve lifeboats were available for use in case of emergency for the total of 554 people. However, as a transport ship she carried around 734 Italian internees (*fascio* Italians), 479 German and Austrian internees, 86 German prisoners of war, 174 officers and crew and from the War Office, 9 officers and 245 military guards, totalling 1,729 – three times her normal capacity, but with the same number of lifeboats. Additional life rafts were loaded to make up the difference in case of an emergency.

Orders were given to start loading. 'The queue started to walk up a gangplank one at time,'[5] said Joe Pieri.

It took around five to six hours to load the *Arandora Star* with her cargo of internees, and once she reached her capacity the queue was stopped and re-directed to go onto the *Ettrick*. Among the 734 Italian men aboard the *Arandora Star* were Ettore Feraboli, Decio Anzani, Nello Cardosi, Uberto Limentani and Gaetano Fracassi; a violin teacher, a tailor, a proprietor, a translator at the BBC and a priest, respectively. There were also men with sons in the British army and men aged in their sixties who did not know how to swim.

As the men boarded the *Arandora Star*, speculation was rife as to their destination: 'Nobody had told the internees where they would be taken,' said Rupert Limentani, 'and the general opinion seemed to be that they were going to the Isle of Man, so they embarked on the *Arandora Star*, thinking that they were going to the Isle of Man.'[6] 'I just carried on obeying orders,' said Rando Betoia; 'the soldiers said, "In here," and off I went – I didn't know where I was going or anything, I knew nothing.'[7]

On boarding the ship, most of the Italians were quartered on Deck A, the main deck, and Deck B, the upper deck. Some 240 German merchant seamen were quartered on Deck D, the promenade deck, and in the ballroom. The remainder, including the ship's escort, may have been quartered on Deck C, the bridge deck, Deck D, the promenade deck, or Deck E, the upper promenade deck. Temporary shelters had been erected on the decks to house another 500 prisoners of war, but these lay empty as embarkation had been denied to those prisoners, either by the Captain of the *Arandora Star* or by Major Bethell, because of how overloaded the *Arandora Star* already was.

Accommodating such a large number of men meant that every area of the ship had to be used for quarters. It would appear that the lower decks with cabins were loaded first. Communal areas, not usually used for quarters, had to be employed too. After the ship had been loaded with internees, more military guards arrived comprising men serving in England, Scotland and Wales. Harold Finney, 20 years of age at the time, was one of them:

> We got to the ship. We couldn't see anybody on board because they'd already got settled in it. We were put on and we were given our cabins, and for a few hours we were organising things, our kit bag and everything, and then got some sleep. We set sail late afternoon, and I was

given a job on watch duty on the corridors on one of the parts of the ship.[8]

Also among the military guard were the 9th Battalion Cameronians (Scottish Rifles), and one of the men in this battalion was Rifleman Peter Tarchetti. It is not clear whether Peter was guarding German, Austrian or Italian internees, but it is easy to imagine that upon seeing the Italian men the thought may have crossed his mind that his father Tranquillo could be on board the ship too, given that most of the men were of a similar age, spoke English and, like Tranquillo, were Italians resident in Britain.

The ship set sail on 30 June 1940. Once aboard, the internees began to take in their new surroundings: '[My father] noticed a few particulars about the ship,' said Rupert Limentani, 'in particular that the lifeboats seemed to be in lousy condition as far as maintenance was concerned and that there was a lot of barbed wire around.'[9]

On 1 July the *Arandora Star* was in the Atlantic Ocean, sailing unescorted. It became obvious to the internees that their destination was further afield than the Isle of Man, despite what many had initially thought, and despondency grew among the older deportees. The ship was armed with a 4.7 inch gun and a 12-pound cannon and was flying a blue ensign with the Admiralty anchor. She was sailing in a No. 10 zigzag pattern – a tactic used by the Admiralty to avoid being torpedoed by a U-boat. A degaussing circuit was operating at the time to reduce the strength of her magnetic field and counter the threat from mines at sea. Her speed was 15 knots. Although the ocean was infested with U-boats, one day into the *Arandora Star*'s voyage danger lay within the ship herself.

The previous night, it had been reported that the 240 German seamen quartered in the ballroom had set up a swastika flag and sung Nazi choruses. This, considering their proximity to the ship's steering arrangements, was thought to constitute a danger.

Among the German and Austrian internees were men who were not just classified as category 'A' internees but also given an 'R', or 'Ringleader', classification. These seamen had been captured on armed merchant ships and therefore were very near the prisoners of war category though not classified as such. In contrast, within the same nationalities were Jewish men who in some cases had been reclassified from category 'B' internees to category 'A'. It is likely that these men were anti-Nazis. Therefore there were huge ideological differences among the Germans and Austrians, and the two nationalities divided themselves into pro- and anti-Nazi groups on the ship.

The matter was discussed in a meeting held on the morning of 1 July attended by Major Bethell, the Officer Commanding, Captain F.J. Robertson, the interpreter to the Italians, and the purser, in order to improve conditions and to raise concerns, including those regarding the German seamen. It was suggested and later agreed that the German seamen should exchange quarters with the Italians, and that this exchange should begin at 1500 hours.

At 1500 hours Captain Robertson began his task of moving the Italians in Decks A and B to the ballroom on Deck D. He was met with protest and threats of resistance but after two hours was able to clear the cabins to prepare for the arrival of the Germans. Captain Lee (the interpreter for the Germans) was doing a similar job with the Germans, meeting some resistance too and some annoyance from the men at their being exposed to the elements on Deck D. At around 1900 hours the Italians went into the ballroom. Captain Robertson had made arrangements for 200 men but was greeted with the arrival of 400 Italians, including some who had mistaken their orders or hoped to get better quarters and had attached themselves to the group. Captain Robertson settled the uproar and hysteria that ensued and calmed the men. He then set about finding additional quarters.

While the Italian orderlies provided dinner, Captain Robertson found the large shed on Sports Deck E, specially erected for 500 prisoners, which lay empty. He was able to persuade some 30 to 40 men to make use of the shed. The rest, like father and son Alfredo and Ettore Giannotti, preferred to remain in the crowded ballroom although, as Captain Robinson pointed out to them, Deck E was much closer to the lifeboats in case of an emergency. After exchanging quarters, the internees acquainted themselves with their new surroundings, ate an evening meal and settled down for the night. Nearly two days into the voyage across the Atlantic, Lieutenant J. F. Constable noted: 'The ship's crew had not been practised in Emergency Station[s]. The Military Personnel and Internees had not been instructed in the use of life jackets or told off to Emergency Stations.'[10]

11

The Last Torpedo

On the morning of 2 July 1940, the *Arandora Star* was 150 miles north-west of Bloody Foreland, County Donegal. Also in the vicinity was U-boat 47, captained by Günther Prien, a U-boat ace who had successfully breached the defences of the base of the British fleet at Scapa Flow in the Orkneys in September 1939 and sunk the *Royal Oak* at anchor with the loss of over 850 men. He was on his way back to base at Wilhelmshaven from a successful patrol in the North Atlantic, having sunk eight allied merchant ships, when the *Arandora Star* came into his sights. Having assessed the *Arandora Star* as a legitimate target, he dived and approached to within 2,500 metres and just before 0700 hours fired his last torpedo.

At about 0445 hours that morning, Captain Robertson had been awakened by the sound of a bugle announcing the changing of the guard. One of the guards on duty awaiting relief was Harold Finney. He had gone on duty at 0200 and should have been relieved at 0400.

However, his relief had not arrived (maybe due to seasickness) and he was still at his post at 0615, after an uneventful night shift. The early morning silence was shattered by a loud noise. 'All of a sudden,' said Harold, 'there was this large explosion, which at first I thought probably it was engine trouble because with it being at the other end of the ship it didn't sound so loud.'[1]

Captain Robertson, who was in his cabin waiting for his tea, felt a sudden shock. The lights went out and he heard the crashing of glass and concluded it to be a minor accident in the engine room. Internee Uberto Limentani initially thought that the *Arandora Star* might have hit an iceberg, although unlikely in July off the Irish coast.

Günther Prien's torpedo had truck the *Arandora Star* in the after end on the starboard side. The explosion had damaged the engine room, and the main generator was put out of action. The upward movement of the explosion had disabled the emergency generator equipment, which meant that the ship had no power and was in complete darkness. It took two minutes for the chief engineer, R.C. Connell, to get from his cabin to the main engine room door on Deck B. When he arrived, the door had been blown off and lay in the working alley. The engine room was already flooded to sea level.

The crashing of glass heard by Captain Robinson was likely to have come from the ballroom, where mirrors attached on the walls fell down on the Italian internees who had been moved there the previous day. Shards and splinters were strewn across the ballroom floor, causing terrible injuries and incapacitating some of the men. Alfredo Giannotti was very badly injured. As others began to leave the ballroom, his son Ettore stayed behind and tried to nurse his father's wounds as best he could.

After initially speculating as to what the noise had been, those furthest from the explosion began to leave their quarters and go up to the open decks. As they did so, the *Arandora Star* took a 5-degree starboard list and the tilt made it evident that the ship was taking in water. The alarms were rung immediately and more internees started to head for the decks. Hundreds of German, Austrian and Italian internees began arriving from within the cabins, the ballroom and the lounge. As an emergency drill had not been performed the previous day, the crew, guards and internees were all in the same position, as Harold Finney, stationed on the deck, explained:

> Along the corridor and down the steps there was a load of internees of all nationalities shaking me and asking me, 'Where are the life belts?' Well I couldn't tell them, I didn't even know about mine, I just saw it on the wall and put it on.[2]

The destination for the internees was the outer decks and then the lifeboats. However, access to some of the boats had not been cleared of barbed wire, and the guards were now finding it difficult to remove. Major Bethell, in charge of the guards and issuing orders to clear the wire, was unaware that there was a special method for loosening sections of the barricades by operating a slip wire, for no instructions on this had been given to him. His troops used bayonets and rifle butts to try to prise away the heavy clamps securing sections of the wire, even tearing at the wire with their bare hands. The launching of the lifeboats was also impeded by lack of space on deck due to the temporary structures built to quarter internees.

Leaving his post, Harold Finney made his way to the lifeboats but was faced with a barricade three metres tall. He managed to scramble over the fence, but those who couldn't had to double back on themselves, enter the ship and go through corridors to stairs on the other side. The impact and then the explosion of the torpedo had smashed lifeboat number 7. The falls and davits on lifeboat number 5 were also damaged. Harold reached lifeboat number 5 as it was being lowered:

> As I got down the other side, a lifeboat was being lowered and I thought, oh, I'll get on the next one, because it was absolutely packed. Well, before I could do anymore, all the ironwork letting this boat down crashed on top of them and I could see all the bodies lying underneath the water there.[3]

The previous day Captain Robinson had managed to persuade about 40 Italian men to stay in a shed on Deck E (the same shed that was hindering the rescue effort), because of the cramped conditions inside the ship. The proximity of the shed to the lifeboats in case of an emergency had been a convincing argument, and the men agreed. It is thought that two of these men were Rando Bertoia and a family friend, who managed to get into the same lifeboat as Captain Robinson. It is likely that the same family friend who at Wharf Mills made the promise to Rando's father to look after his son Rando kept his word in the ensuing disaster.

> One of my friends saw me going around aimlessly, so they were in a wee boat, in a lifeboat, so I slipped through the bars there and he grabbed me and pulled me through. So, I went on to the boat, I was very lucky they put me on that, and the thing went down quite nicely, it latched a wee bit because the thing was not in good order and it landed on the surface very well, so from then there were oars there and people pulled the oars and we tried to get away from the ship as much as we could, aye ... aye, so from there the disaster carried on.[4]

In the ensuing confusion, the German merchant seamen appeared to cope best. The Italians, especially many of the older men, had come from mountain areas in Italy and didn't know how to swim. Rather than trying to leave the ship, some of these men held on to the rails, hoping that the ship would not sink.

Uberto Limentani had managed to make his way along the dark corridor from the interior of the ship and had decided to get to the highest point. Dismissing the possibility of a place in a lifeboat, Uberto's thoughts turned to abandoning the stricken vessel. In his mind the *Arandora Star* was sinking and it was time to leave. His son Rupert explained how he did this:

> His [Dad's] next thought was, 'What's the best way to abandon ship so as not to incur an injury?' having seen that people who simply leapt off one of the decks were in many cases seriously injured when they landed in the water because they hit some pieces of debris or because the jump was simply too high. I mean, jumping off E deck was like jumping out of the fourth floor of a building, and it's something that can seriously injure somebody who is not a practised diver. So he found himself first a piece of rope but then, dissatisfied with that, found himself a rope step ladder and climbed down this into the water on his own.[5]

As the ship took on more and more water, the sense of urgency among the men increased. Relatives who had been separated by the initial arrests, then reunited at Wharf Mills, were again separated in the ensuing tragedy. Angelo Albericci was with his brother on the *Arandora Star* but they were separated soon after the torpedo struck. His daughter Angela wrote:

> My father could not swim, but he eventually found a life belt. He was too late for a lifeboat so climbed down a rope and jumped into the sea, knowing he must try to get as far away from the ship as possible ... he was plucked out of the sea by a German sailor. This sailor wanted a fourth man to balance the raft he and two others were sitting on, two men back to back with another two.[6]

About 90 life rafts were carried on the upper deck. More than half of these were thrown overboard, but as the ship had not come to a complete stop these rafts were rendered useless. Once the ship had stopped, the remainder of the rafts were thrown overboard and some struck men already in the water. Men also caused terrible injuries to themselves by sliding down ropes into the ocean, burning the palms of their hands. Those who had made a successful descent into the Atlantic began to distance themselves from the stricken liner and found pieces of debris to hold on to. Uberto Limentani set about trying to get away, as Rupert explained:

> His [Dad's] main preoccupation at the time was to swim as far away from the *Arandora Star* as possible so as not to be sucked down when the ship itself went down ... with a piece of wood acting as a support, he swam further and further away from the ship, although he said that he couldn't resist turning round to see what was happening ... the horrible, fascinating spectacle of it gradually going down.[7]

The gun was torn from its mooring and crashed into the sea, followed by a trail of barbed wire, hooking further victims into the Atlantic. The funnels that gave life to the engine below them broke from their fixings and crashed into the sea, and the ship's boilers exploded. The Chief Officer of the *Arandora Star*, F. Brown, recalled the final moments of the ship:

It was apparent that she was about to sink, it was then that the Captain and Senior Officers walked over the side, many of the Italian internees still refused to leave. I was picked up by a boat after being in the water about 20 minutes ... the vessel turned over and sank stern first almost immediately and I think that they [Captain, officers and Italians] must have been trapped as she came over.[8]

The last three people to been seen on deck were Captain Moulton, Father Fracassi, an interned Italian priest, and Captain Otto Burfeind. Günther Prien, having seen the lifeboats lowered and the *Arandora Star* submerge into the ocean, continued on his way to base, adding another several thousand tons to his already successful campaign.

12

Rescue

'It was terrible,' said Rando Bertoia, having watched from a lifeboat the final moments before the *Arandora Star* sank. 'Everything was quiet after all the carry on, everything was quiet, a very uncanny and a very eerie quiet. There was just sky and water to see.'[1]

Around half an hour had passed from the time that Günther Prien's last torpedo had struck the *Arandora Star* to the moment that the Atlantic Ocean claimed the 15,000-ton liner. Her contents of internees, lifeboats, life rafts and debris were scattered and floating in all directions on the surface of the water. Uberto Limentani, adrift on a floating table with another survivor, spotted a lifeboat on the horizon and concentrated his efforts on swimming towards it. After two hours, he eventually reached the lifeboat and called for help, in Italian. His son Rupert continued:

> He shouted out, 'Aiuto [help],' and a number of the passengers on board said, 'No, we can't take on Italians, we can only take on British survivors.' They were

overruled by the second in command [third officer] of the
Arandora Star, Mr Tulip, who said, 'No, we're at sea. At
sea, any survivor has to be rescued independently of
where he comes from so you take him on board.' So he
was taken on and shoved under with two or three people
sitting on top of him and he said that he managed to find
a seaman's jacket to wrap around himself to keep himself
warm.[2]

Captain Robertson was also on a lifeboat, picking up
survivors from the thick oil that had spread on the surface
of the water. This lifeboat was taking in water, and those on
board, soldiers and Italians, took turns at bailing and
rowing.

By now several hours had passed and the time was
approaching midday. The Atlantic Ocean began to stir and
swell. Many survivors, both in the lifeboats and on the rafts,
suffered from violent seasickness. Men who had been
injured in the sinking, as well as many who had been in the
water since the ship sank, began to lose the fight for life.
The bodies of the dead were pushed over the sides and
replaced by those still in the sea who were alive. In this
despondent time, the whir of an aeroplane engine pierced

the sombre atmosphere and the shipwrecked men turned their eyes skywards. A British Sunderland flying boat appeared overhead and began circling the scene of the disaster. Rando Bertoia felt an overwhelming sense of relief upon seeing the plane:

> It was an enemy plane, but anyway the enemy was a 'good' enemy and it threw down foodstuffs for us to keep us going. So after that, well it just went away to its base, but we knew then that we were located, so I was quite happy then.[3]

The plane relayed the survivors' location and radioed a local ship to rescue them. Help came in the form of a Canadian destroyer, the HMCS *St Laurent*, commanded by Captain Wolf. Upon seeing the ship, those in lifeboats began to row towards its safety. In his report of proceedings, Captain Wolf described the scene that he and his crew found and the enormity of the task that lay ahead:

> On reaching the position, ten lifeboats, apparently well filled, were visible, somewhat scattered, while the area to windward [westward] for two or three miles, was littered

with rafts and light wreckage, to which were clinging many survivors, singly, and in small groups. The sea was calm with a slight confused swell, the wind light variable westerly. The temperature of the sea was 55° F [12.7° C]. The ship was stopped in the centre of this area of wreckage, and all boats sent away with instructions to pick up individuals from the water, and those with poor support, while the ship was manoeuvred among the rafts and heavier wreckage picking up groups of three or four. This part of the work was painfully slow. Very few survivors were able to help themselves to any extent, and in many cases it was necessary to have a man over the side to pass a line around them and hoist them bodily inboard. Some were very heavy. Many of those taken from the water and from light wreckage were covered in oil fuel.[4]

With the help of the Sunderland flying boat pointing out distant individual survivors, the *St Laurent* was able to rescue approximately 850 survivors. The men were given rum, a cigarette and a blanket, and treated as shipwrecked men rather than as enemy aliens. At around 1555 hours the last of the boats had been cleared and the Sunderland flying boat was given permission to return to base.

Family members that had been separated during the disaster were reunited: 'On board the destroyer my father found his brother safe and unharmed – he had been one of the fortunate ones to get into a lifeboat,'[5] wrote Angelo Albericci's daughter.

More than 850 extra men had to be quartered on the *St Laurent*, and every conceivable part of ship was used, as Captain Wolf described:

> As many survivors as could be were stowed below, filling all messes, Officers' quarters and one Boiler Room, but a number were obliged to remain on deck and were made as comfortable as possible with canvas screens. Armed sentries were posted, and each space occupied by internees also contained a number of military guard survivors, but no difficulty was experienced. The internees generally appeared grateful for what they were getting and many of them made every effort to assist.[6]

Maintaining its high speed, the *St Laurent* reached the safety of Greenock on the river Clyde in Scotland on the morning of 3 July. Such was the kindness, compassion and bravery shown towards those from the *Arandora Star*, and so great the incredible feat of fitting all the survivors, including several stretcher cases, on board the *St Laurent*, and feeding and comforting them as well, that when the ship reached Greenock, all the individual groups who had been rescued showed their gratitude, by giving the crew of the *St Laurent* three cheers.

The scale of the rescue carried out by the *St Laurent* was one of the largest for allied shipping during the war. The *St Laurent* rescued 119 crew members, 163 military guards, 243 Italians, and 343 Germans and Austrians. Unfortunately, the loss of life was also one of the highest of the entire war for allied shipping.

News of the sinking of the *Arandora Star* reached the War Cabinet on 3 July 1940. At a meeting held in the morning they agreed that the sinking of the *Arandora Star* should not interfere with the policy of deportation agreed by the Cabinet before the disaster and that the remainder of the ships carrying internees should leave as scheduled. That same day the *Ettrick* set sail from Liverpool for Canada. News of the disaster was published the following day in the national newspapers.

13

'Missing Presumed Drowned'

At the Feraboli household in Clapham, South London, the arresting detectives had told Tina and Graziella that Ettore would be gone for a few days. A few days passed, but there was no news of him, so Graziella and her mother went to the police station to make enquiries:

> We didn't know where he was, so frantic phone calls all over the place. The Italian embassy was closed, the police knew nothing, and I'm sure they knew nothing, they didn't know where they'd taken him – the local police I mean, that had arrested him, detained him – I'm sure they didn't know where he had gone. He'd been sent off somewhere we didn't know, nobody knew ... and there were hundreds of other Italian families in London sharing the same fate. We telephoned round to a lot of friends and they said the same story, 'My husband was taken away in the morning and we don't know where he is.' And then there were three nightmarish weeks in which we just didn't know where to turn. We were running round in circles.[1]

On 4 July 1940, news was beginning to be broadcast on the radio and printed in the newspapers about a ship called the *Arandora Star*, which had been torpedoed and sunk in the Atlantic Ocean. The *Daily Telegraph* was delivered to the Feraboli household; the front page read '*Arandora Star* sunk by U-boat, one thousand five hundred Italian and Nazi internees in panic', 'Fight for lifeboats hampers rescues', 'Captain and officers last seen on Bridge'.[2] The paper went on:

> A panic among one thousand five hundred German and Italian internees being taken to Canada in the fifteen thousand, five hundred and one ton Leyland liner *Arandora Star* heavily increased the death toll when the vessel was torpedoed and sunk by a German submarine three hundred miles off the west coast of Ireland. About one thousand scantily clad survivors were landed at a Scottish west coast port yesterday from a British ship. The liner was not in convoy at the time she was sunk. The owners state that a considerable proportion of the crew were saved. The greater part of the drowned internees appear to have been Italians, most of whom had been traders in this country.[3]

Graziella and her mother had received a letter from Ettore from Wharf Mills internment camp in Britain. However, when they read the article they feared the worst – that he had been deported and might have been on the *Arandora Star*:

> It was a horrendous report of the sinking of the *Arandora Star*... After which my mother, being a very practical person, gathered things together and said, 'We have to start getting information,' which was the last thing we could find because nobody knew anything. More phone calls because other people had read the news but nobody knew anything.[4]

The Italian embassy was closed and its responsibilities had been taken over by the Brazilian and Swiss embassies. The War and Home offices drew up lists of people who had been lost. Women trying to find out whether their loved ones had embarked on the *Arandora Star* made their way to the Brazilian embassy. Graziella and her mother made the journey to try to establish Ettore's whereabouts:

We rushed there and we found an enormous queue of Italian women outside, all eager for news … and one at a time we were shown into an office. We had to give the name and number of the prisoner as he was called and there was just a very, very short reply, 'Missing presumed drowned.' Well, I didn't even understand what it meant, but when it dawned on me, I mean after a moment's silence … my mother said nothing, and I just shouted out, 'You've … what have you done to him, you've killed him? Is that what you mean?' and my mother took me by the arm and got me outside. Outside there were scenes of despair, there were women shouting, crying, fainting … one or two fainted … because most of the answers had been the same as ours.[5]

The exact death toll from the *Arandora Star* was difficult to ascertain, with different government departments giving different figures, but at least 838 men perished in the disaster, among them the captain, 12 officers, 42 crewmen, 94 guards, 243 Germans and 446 Italians. Of the 446 Italians lost, most were men who called Britain home. The news of the tragedy began to arrive in the homes of their families in England, Scotland and Wales as it had for Tina and Graziella.

Liliana Cortesio was born in London on 7 January 1931. Her father Giovanni was from the Savigliano province of Cunio, near Turin. He was born in 1899 and went to London just after the First World War. He met and married Liliana's mother in London and they lived in Clapham. By 1940, after working in various restaurants, he was manager of the Monseigneur Restaurant in London.

After seeing her father arrested at their home in Clapham on 11 June 1940, and having had no news from him for several weeks, Liliana returned from school one afternoon in early July to find her mother and a family friend crying in the living room. The family friend had gone to the Brazilian embassy and had received the news that her husband was 'missing presumed drowned', along with Liliana's father Giovanni:

> I came home, I could see that my mother had been crying
> a little bit but I wasn't the type to sort of ... ask questions.
> My Aunt Laura, she wasn't really my aunt but my mother
> was friends with her and the family, they were like two
> sisters, she lost her husband as well and they'd obviously
> been talking about it.[6]

Liliana's father was one of several hoteliers and caterers lost on the *Arandora Star*. Names of men missing presumed drowned were included in publications within the catering industry. In an article published in *The Caterer and Hotel Keeper* on 12 July 1940, a list of men who worked in the hotels and restaurants of London's West End was included. Among the names were Italo Zangiacomi, general manager of the Piccadilly Hotel; Cesare Maggi, restaurant manager of the Ritz Hotel; Joseph Benini, manager of the Hungaria Restaurant; John (Giovanni) Sovrani, manager of the Normandie Hotel, Knightsbridge; Cesare Borgo, manager of the Café Anglais; Hector (Ettore) Zavattoni, banqueting manager of the Savoy Hotel; Primo Pozzo, chef at the Monseigneur Restaurant; and Magno Boscasso, manager of Hatchetts Restaurant, Piccadilly.

In Wales, Clementina Cordani and her mother had taken in an Italian lady, Mrs Spania, who had lived in an alien restricted area and was asked to leave under the order. The Cordanis were category 'B' enemy aliens and lived under restriction, including the confiscation of their radio, and so it was their British neighbour, Mrs Rogers, who broke the news of the *Arandora Star*:

She [Mrs Rogers] said one of the Italian ships had been sunk, been torpedoed. Is my father on there? My uncle? Are they on another ship? We didn't know a thing and we didn't know for a good week before the police came to tell us that my father and my uncle were all right [interned on the Isle of Man] but Mr Spania was on the *Arandora Star* and God, you know, I can remember Mrs Spania going to her bedroom and locking herself in, she wouldn't open the door. They got in contact with one of her cousins and he came to fetch her because she had gone to pieces.[7]

The Home Office later sent official notification to the victims' families by post. Liliana Cortesio and her mother received a letter:

It is with deep regret that the Secretary of State directs me to inform you that since a certain 'G. Cortesio' No. 58122 appears on the lists as sailing on the *Arandora Star*, on the 30th June 1940, and has not been subsequently recorded on the embarkation lists of internees, who have left this country for Canada or Australia, or among those detained in internments camps in this country, he must be presumed missing and probably lost.[8]

Some families received two of these letters; the Giannottis received one for Alfredo (father) and another for Ettore (son). The letters offered no explanation as to why they had been deported. The families that had witnessed the arrest of male relatives assumed that they would be interned in Britain, rather than deported to camps abroad. Within a short period of time it started to emerge that the victims included Italians who had been resident in Britain all their lives, and also that there were anti-fascists among them.

The sinking of the *Arandora Star* was raised in the House of Commons on 10 July 1940 and the House of Lords on 6 August. To quell the criticisms, on 5 August Churchill instructed Lord Snell to hold an inquiry into the method of selection of aliens sent overseas in the *Arandora Star*. Lord Snell's summary of the *Arandora Star* inquiry was presented to the Cabinet in November 1940. He found:

In the case of the Italians, no classification by tribunals had taken place and there was no alternative but to work on such material as was already available ... the responsibility for the compilation of lists of dangerous Italians rested with the security authorities, and as time did not permit further scrutiny these lists were accepted as being the equivalent of the Category 'A' Germans and Austrians. The lists were largely based on membership of the Fascist Party, which was the only evidence against many of these persons. Apparently the view was taken that those who had been only nominal members of the Fascist Party and those who were ardently Fascist were equally dangerous. The result was that among those deported were a number of men whose sympathies were wholly with this country. One of the Italians deported had lived in England for twenty years and had been included in the list in error; he was not a member of the Fascist Party. Lord Snell could not regard this lack of discrimination as satisfactory and held that the security authorities must bear some of the responsibility for the results which followed from the acceptance of their list as a reliable list of 'dangerous characters'.[9]

In summary, Lord Snell concluded that some errors had been made, but given the urgency and the pressure under which the work had been carried out he did not consider that the number of errors was a cause for serious criticism. Diplomats in the Foreign Office claimed that the report was a whitewash of the matter. The Italian described by Lord Snell was Decio Anzani. He was a tailor with a workshop in Mayfair and been resident in Britain for 31 years. He was secretary of the Italian League for the Rights of Man, opposed to Mussolini's fascist regime. The League produced and distributed anti-fascist leaflets. His daughter Renée was left completely incensed by his inclusion on a list of persons thought to pose a danger to the safety of Britain.

Nominal fascist membership applied to most of the men. Nello Cardosi, his wife and two small children went to the London *fascio* to use some of the facilities there such as the school and social clubs for the children. He had turned down the Ambassador's offer of repatriation to Italy because his family and property was in Britain. Graziella Feraboli's father Ettore had lived in London since the First World War, had married and was raising a daughter in the city. He had a studio at the London *fascio*, where he taught violin. This was the sum of his subversive activities. Other men whose selection for deportation was questionable included Gaetano Pacitto, a naturalised British subject from Hull, 65 years of age, and Francesco D'Ambrosio, confectioner and restaurateur from Hamilton, Scotland, who had applied for naturalisation, had two sons serving in the British army and was 68 years of age.

Some families tried to claim compensation. The family of Giuseppe Del Grosso, originally from Borgotaro, Emilia-Romagna, but living in Hamilton and working in the ice cream trade, was one such. After his body was washed ashore on the Island of Colonsay in the Inner Hebrides, north of Islay and south of Mull, the family hired a solicitor to act on their behalf. On 20 December 1940, the solicitors W.M. & J.C. Pollok pressed a claim for compensation to the Rt. Hon. Secretary of State for Home Affairs, arguing:

> A serious mistake had been made which resulted in Mr Delgrosso being deported. So far as we know, there was no reason why he should have been, unless that he was Italian is considered a valid reason. By his death, the widow and family, the latter are Scottish born and British, have suffered a very severe loss. We submit on their behalf a claim for compensation and reparation for the loss so sustained. We will be pleased to hear from you

that the government accept the responsibility of compensating those so tragically bereaved.[10]

A request for the return of money, a gold watch and finger ring (likely to have been confiscated by police when he was first arrested) and compensation were also included. On 9 January 1941, a division of the Home Office, directed by the Secretary of State, wrote back to the solicitors saying:

> The Secretary of State sympathises with the relatives of Mr Delgrosso in their loss but he regrets that he cannot entertain a claim for compensation in that regard. The 'Arandora Star' is known to have been sunk on the high seas by enemy torpedo without warning, contrary to the well recognised rules of warfare and His Majesty's Government could not admit the principle of paying compensation in respect of interned aliens who lost their lives through the barbarous act of an enemy government.[11]

After Giuseppe's body was washed ashore on Colonsay, it was buried by some of the islanders. It is thought that the body was later returned to his family in Hamilton, Scotland.

On 25 October 1940, following hospitalisation, 42 Italian survivors were taken to the Metropole Camp on the Isle of Man for internment. Having survived the disaster and after receiving treatment for his injuries at Means Kirk emergency hospital, Uberto Limentani was released from Donaldson Internment Camp, on application to the Home Office by the BBC. His son Rupert explained:

> He was the first prisoner to be released from that internment camp and a soldier took him personally by tram to Edinburgh train station and put him on a train to London, and the next day he was back at the BBC at the microphone.[12]

For the families of the 243 survivors, who did not receive the news 'missing presumed drowned', the next task was to find out where their loved ones were. A list of survivors had not been published by the Home Office because the internees were still category 'A' regardless of their general situation, and public knowledge of their location would be a threat to security. It was later left to other organisations like the church to help the internees send news to their families that they were still alive. Through their families' letterboxes across the country, postcards and letters began to arrive from the survivors themselves. Angelo Albericci was able to send news to his family through the church. His daughter Angela remembered learning that he was alive:

> We heard that they [father and father's brother] were both safe – I think through the good offices of a Vatican agency dealing with refugees. It was just a brief card stating, 'Angelo and Santo both safe and well.'[13]

Although the initial attempt by the government to deport the men had ended in disaster, they continued with their policy. Those rescued and not hospitalised were again transferred to Liverpool Docks to be deported. However, the final ship to be used for deportation was destined not for Canada but for Australia. Just eight days after their terrifying ordeal in the Atlantic, the survivors of the *Arandora Star* were embarked on another ship. On 10 July 1940 the SS *Dunera* sailed for Australia. On board were 2,288 Jewish refugees, and 244 German and 200 Italian survivors from the *Arandora Star.* Along with other personnel, the total on board was 2,873 men.

14

The Dominions

The day after the sinking of the *Arandora Star* in the
Atlantic Ocean, a cargo of 900 prisoners of war, 1,300
German and Austrian internees and 403 single Italian men,
including Joe Pieri, set sail aboard the *Ettrick*, an 11,000-ton
troopship, in a similar fashion. The *Ettrick* was provided
with a destroyer escort for the first 36 hours. None of the
internees knew where the ship was going. After seeing the
size of the *Ettrick* and being quartered in a hold, rumours
began to circulate among the internees as to their
destination. Speculation was that it would be the Isle of
Man, but eventually the internees found that they were
bound for North America. After leaving Liverpool on the 3
July and crossing the Atlantic Ocean the *Ettrick* docked in
Quebec on 15 July 1940, 12 days after leaving Liverpool
Docks.

The internees were transferred onto trains and
finally buses, which took them to their camp in Montreal. It
appeared to Joe that the Canadians were expecting mainly

German-speaking prisoners and internees:

There were signs in the camp and they were written in German. Nobody [internees] understood German and the guards got the impression that we were being stubborn and that we weren't obeying the orders and we took a few knocks. Anyhow, we were assembled in groups of 20, seated on the ground, and it took about a couple of hours for all the buses to be unloaded and orders and questions were being shouted out in German until finally one of our group, a fellow called Ralph Taglione who was manager of the Café Royal in London, Regents Street, I remember he put up his hand and said, 'Please sir, nobody here speaks German.' So the officer said, 'Well what bloody language do you speak?' He [Ralph] says, 'Well, we all speak English, we're English here, I'm from London, some are here from Scotland.' The officer's jaw dropped, then he turned round and he spoke to another officer and they conferred with other officers and then after that, treatment changed dramatically. We were no longer kicked, no longer shoved, no longer nudged with rifle butts. We were given orders brusquely but not a finger was laid on us.[1]

The newly arrived internees were given a blue uniform with a red patch on the back. Their hair was shaved off. They were given a number and interviewed. Expecting dangerous characters, the Canadian authorities found instead that most of the Italian men from Britain were in the catering industry and worked in chip shops, spaghetti houses and ice cream shops. For the majority of the Italian internees who were deported to Canada in July 1940, Camp 43 in Montreal would be home for the next three years.

The Italian men on the *Ettrick* were the last names to be selected for deportation. Deportation of Italian men to the dominions stopped after arrangements began to be discussed by the British and Italian governments to exchange Italian internees for British Citizens in Italy. All future shipments to the dominions were composed of German and Austrian category 'B' and 'C' aliens.

Many months passed before the authorities informed relatives of the aliens' destination, but Joe managed to send word back to his parents much sooner. Aboard the *Ettrick* were guards with Glaswegian accents.

Joe spoke to one of the guards who knew Joe's fish and chip shop. He asked the guard if he'd mind letting his parents know that he'd been deported to Canada:

> Believe it or not, about six weeks after that he must have got leave and he went and he told my parents that he had met their son on a ship going to Canada. So they knew before they were officially informed by the Red Cross, because they went to the police station and they would give them no information as to where I was. Anyhow, they were eventually put on to the International Red Cross and I would say that official notification was given of my whereabouts maybe about four months after we had landed in Montreal, and then I began to get Red Cross parcels, but for a good period of time the families of those on the *Ettrick* had no idea where their sons were.[2]

As the initial rough treatment of this group of internees, whom the Canadian authorities had expected to be 'dangerous characters' but turned out to be harmless shopkeepers, subsided, the men settled themselves into their new surroundings:

You got used to the strict discipline of the camp. You were up at a certain time, you got counted, you got fed, and you volunteered for work if you wanted to. Everywhere you went you were under guard with fixed bayonets; you weren't allowed to have any contact with civilians. Life in the camp was very, very strict, it wasn't an internment camp but it was a POW [prisoner of war] camp run along POW lines.[3]

Discipline was more stringent in these camps as the Canadian authorities had also received genuinely dangerous characters. Unlike those on the Isle of Man, internees in Canada were category 'A' and therefore not allowed visitors. As most of their relatives were in Britain it is unlikely any would risk the journey or that the government would have the shipping to make such arrangements.

Within the government grouping of German, Austrian and Italian were men with nothing in common other than the label that had been attached to them. In the group of 403 Italians were individuals who were vastly different from one another. Joe noticed natural divisions and suspicions among them, especially between the Italians from Italy and the Italians from Britain:

> We had 150 sailors who were 'pure Italian' and they were all fascist and they looked upon us as, here are people that speak two languages, they can speak to the guards because they speak English among themselves, some of them don't speak Italian, so there was already a division within the camp, us versus the sailors ... the tension in the camp was, well, quite unbearable really.[4]

To ease these tensions and relieve boredom, various activities were organised. In the camp were academics who specialised in different fields, and classes were organised for internees to attend. Having left school at the age of 14 to work in the family's fish and chip shop, Joe took the opportunity to expand his mind:

> For me, the camp, I call it my college days. In the camp we had lots of academics and lots of university people. We had professors of English, professors of Italian. We had some schoolteachers and they set up classes and I attended every class I could ... and I say that's where I got my education, such as it is. I tried to put it to good use; I

learned to speak German. I broadened my knowledge of everything, I began to realise that the world didn't consist just of a fish and chip shop but there were other things out there.[5]

As with internees sent to the Isle of Man, the Home Office acknowledged that mistakes had been made in deporting some of the Italians to Canada. A Home Office Commissioner called Alexander Patterson was sent by the British government to investigate conditions in the Canadian Camps and assess individual cases. He arrived on 25 November 1940. Joe didn't go to see Patterson:

Why didn't I go? Looking back, I suppose I had a chip on my shoulder. I felt I had been badly treated; I had been arrested for no good reason. A lot of them who went for an interview were given release provided they joined the British army. Well, at that time my sentiments towards the British army weren't all that great in view of the fact of the way I had been treated, so I didn't even go to see him.[6]

Joe waited for events to unfold in the war, and three years later, after Italy capitulated in August 1943, he left Canada in November, crossing the Atlantic in convoy homeward bound for Glasgow.

Several thousand miles away, but interned under similar conditions, were the survivors of the *Arandora Star*. Originally destined for Canada, they had been deported to Australia on the *Dunera*. On boarding the ship, the internees were punched, kicked and prodded with rifle butts, and received a verbal assault of abusive language. Any valuables were confiscated, and what the guards didn't want was thrown away. The *Dunera* was a converted troopship built to carry 2,000; she sailed with 2,873.

As the *Dunera* was over capacity, the *Arandora Star* survivors had to be quartered in a mess deck with wooden tables and chairs fixed to the floor. The furniture was used to eat and sleep on, with internees lying on the floor, under the tables, on the tables themselves and on the wooden seats. To cope with the overcrowded and awkward conditions, a few hammocks were tied up where possible. The ship was not equipped to carry such a large number of men, and very soon latrines and washbasins became blocked and overflowed, and dysentery broke out among the internees. Malnutrition and weight loss was rife. The main concern for the survivors was being torpedoed again; this happened twice, but the torpedoes missed their target and exploded away from the ship.

Throughout the voyage, the mistreatment of internees continued. When the *Dunera* docked at Fremantle in Western Australia on 7 September, after a 60-day voyage, a party of Australian officers carried out a detailed inspection of the prisoners and their quarters. They registered their disapproval with the commanding officer. The mistreatment of the internees did not go unpunished, and in May and June 1941 three British Officers from the *Dunera*, including Lieutenant Colonel Scott, were court-martialled. A sergeant major was found guilty on ten charges of theft and given one year in prison; a sergeant was found guilty of disobeying a superior officer and reprimanded. The British government paid out £30,000 in compensation to the men who had been on the *Dunera*.

Like the Canadian authorities, the Australians were expecting dangerous characters and the internees were met accordingly. Armed sentries patrolled the dock area and machine gun crews were stationed on the roof of the train waiting to transport them to the camps. However, when the sentries saw that the prisoners were mostly elderly men, doubts began to rise regarding the reports they had read in the press about fifth columnists, parachutists and saboteurs. After some trepidation following events on the *Dunera*, relations between internees and guards became relatively relaxed, with cigarettes being shared out by the guards.

Eventually the train pulled in to No. 2 Internment Camp in Tatura, a town 17 kilometres west of Shepparton in Victoria. On arrival, the internees were each given a palliasse, which they filled with straw, and were issued with two blankets. On the following day, denims, boots, socks, underwear, shirts and pullovers were supplied, together with army coats dyed red with a white patch on the back. After a while it was possible for the internees to write home to send word to their relatives and loved ones of their whereabouts and health.

John Moruzzi was able to send a card to his wife Maria in London. They had been married for about a year when he was arrested and deported. She had received no news directly from John and knew many women who had lost their husbands on the *Arandora Star*, and she was gravely concerned about him. In December 1940 a card was delivered through Maria's letter box: 'I received a card on Christmas Day – they used to deliver the post even on Christmas Day then. His signature was on it with the words "I am well". He couldn't write much because they were small cards.'[7]

She would receive and send many more cards and letters during the five years of her husband's internment in Australia.

The internees settled in to a life behind barbed wire, and many found productive occupations and hobbies to fill their time. Some cultivated small vegetable gardens, the produce of which went to the kitchens to supplement rations. One man set himself up as the camp barber and two others as tailors. Two worked as carpenters, carrying out minor repairs in the camp. Language classes and other learning activities were set up and became very popular. Rando Bertoia made the most of the language classes. Speaking only dialect from his village of origin, Montereale Valcellina, in the province of Pordenone in the Friuli-

Venezia Giulia region of Italy, he took the opportunity to learn Italian among other things:

> We always spoke dialect here [Glasgow] in the house, but in Australia there were one or two teachers there and they were very good and I started off from scratch. I learned Italian, so I was quite bright there, learning the Italian language; that was very good. Then there was other people showed me how to do drawings, and there was one or two people, they were very clever and I just learned one or two wee things there. I was quite happy. There were people who didn't do anything, but I couldn't sit there and do nothing, I had to do something. I made a wee steam engine, scissors and a ring, believe it or not out of a florin ... The one I made was really a good one because it had 1920 on it – that's when I was born, and I asked a soldier to get me one in Australia. They were very friendly, the soldiers, so he brought it up and I made a beautiful ring and it had 1920 inside. It was against the law to deface florins, and one of the guards, it was the camp commandant, saw me and I thought I'm going to be court-martialled here or something, but he didn't mind, he said, 'Carry on, don't worry.'[8]

Along with Rando Bertoia in No. 2 Internment Camp, Tatura, were Angelo and Santo Albericci. The two brothers had survived the sinking of the *Arandora Star* and the perilous journey on the *Dunera*, where they were confined below decks and would not have had a chance to escape if a torpedo had struck. However, the treatment they were receiving in the camp at Tatura was very different. Unlike in Leeds and Manchester, where their families were, there was no rationing in the Australian camp. The two brothers put their skills to use and were mess orderlies along with several other men. Angelo later worked for the Australian Forestry Commission as a member of the wood-cutting team in the bush, earning a little money for his labour. After the Japanese attacked Pearl Harbor in December 1941, the internees in Australia were told to pack their belongings in readiness to move out of Victoria to another camp, No. 10 Internment Camp at Loveday, in South Australia. Here, several unsuccessful attempts to escape were made.

As the Second World War continued into its third year, the British government continued to draft new recruits to serve their country. Some of the internees in

Australia had British-born sons who by now had reached military age. In late 1943 and early 1944, Santo and Angelo Albericci's sons, John and Peter respectively, were called up into the British army. John served in the Royal Army Medical Corps. Peter was sent to the Pioneer Corps, and served in the Orkney Islands. He was transferred to the Royal Army Electrical and Mechanical Engineers (REME), then to the Yorkshire Light Infantry, where the expectation was that he would be going to the Far East. However, the war with Japan came to a sudden end with the dropping of atomic bombs on Hiroshima and Nagasaki, and he was transferred to the Pay Corps and served in Rome and Trieste. Peter thought that perhaps he could have made a case for not joining up, but he felt it might help his father's position if he showed willing to be part of the British war effort. He suffered no discrimination during his service.

As was the case with the Isle of Man and Canada, the Home Office sent a representative to look into the possibility of internees returning to England. Major (later Colonel) Layton was sent to Australia and held tribunals, and any Italian who wished to could apply for a hearing. After collecting all the relevant information, Layton assessed each individual case. However, as in Canada, there were divisions within the internees as to those who were apolitical, those who were pro-fascist and those who were anti-fascist. The fascists looked upon those who chose to apply for a tribunal with suspicion. They behaved in an intimidating way in the camp to prevent internees from going to see Layton, as Rando Bertoia explained:

> I remember a wee clique you know … and there was one who used to take down the names of people who he thought maybe were a wee bit anti-fascist … and so he says, 'When Italy wins the war they will be punished.' When they came along you couldn't say very much because they bullied you so I never bothered. I just kept my mouth shut … you're always afraid to say anything.[9]

After holding the tribunals, Layton contacted London for final approval. If release was granted, it was left to individuals to decide whether to risk the long and dangerous voyage back. Over a period of time, quite a number of internees were released and returned to the United Kingdom. These departures came to a sudden stop when several ships were sunk with loss of life in the Pacific

Ocean: 'Some did try to get back,' said Rando, 'and some of them did get sunk [torpedoed] so I said I'm not taking the chance.'[10] After this tragedy, Rando and many other internees preferred to see out the war in Australia.

15

Homeward Bound

On 7 May 1945, the Second World War in Europe ended with the unconditional surrender of Germany to the Allies, and 14 August saw the end of the war with Japan, which surrendered after the dropping of atomic bombs on the cities of Hiroshima and Nagasaki. Men who had served in the armed forces and were stationed abroad began their return journies home to their families in Britain. Among the vast numbers of service personnel were men returning from internment camps in the Isle of Man, Canada and Australia. Although some Italian men had been released when Italy capitulated in 1943, many remained in the camps until the end of hostilities and all would have to rebuild their lives in a country they called home but which had interned them for being 'enemy aliens'. Reintegrating into society presented many challenges.

The government had released some Italian men just a few months after their arrest in June 1940, realising that among the so-called enemy aliens were men whose sympathies lay with Britain or who were so old that they could pose no threat. Reintegrating into their home lives would have presented the fewest problems for them. Some of the other men were released upon the cessation of hostilities between Italy and Britain, but with the country still at war with Germany and Japan. Others had returned to their lives in Britain only after having been shipped to Canada and spending three years in a prisoner of war camp, or having survived not only the sinking of the *Arandora Star* but also a harrowing 60-day voyage to Australia and internment for five years. Of those sent to camps on the Isle of Man, several hundred had been released by Sir Percy Lorraine in 1940, but several hundred more were interned on the Island for around four years.

The men who returned home in 1943 with the war still raging tried to help the British war effort in whatever way they could. Ernie Mellardi, who had rejoined his young family in Wales at this time, volunteered as a firewatcher. These were men who, when the air raid sirens sounded, would head for the highest point in the village or town in which they lived and signal if incendiary bombs started fires. Wearing tin hats, they would often risk their lives by climbing into tall buildings such as church towers. After Italy's capitulation in 1943 and her joining the Allies, Italian men were no longer enemy aliens and were therefore eligible for release. To many, the news of their release was a shock and a surprise after four years interned behind barbed wire. Dino Viazzani was one such internee:

> We had a tribunal, and after a couple of months the camp commandant Lt. Lipton sent for me. He said to me, 'I've decided to send you home.' I said, 'What? Send me home, after four years you're sending me home, really you're sending me home?' 'I'm sending you home.' I got to the house, Ernie was there, Luis Sidoli his brother and all the rest from Bardi [same origin], I said, 'I'm going home in a few days.' 'What! You're going home? What, you have been released?' 'Yes.' 'How?' 'Eh, I've been released.' 'I don't believe you!' 'Oh,' I said, 'I've been released,' and finally they did. The morning came when I left, they were all crying, all my friends, I left them all behind, and went home.[1]

In 1944 Albert Cavalli became eligible for release, and his four years of internment ended. Aliens like Albert's father were released directly from the Isle of Man but those like Albert, with dual nationality, weren't free until they got to Liverpool and were then released by the police. There were conditions attached to Albert's release, including being barred from certain jobs and being made to make regular visits to the police station:

> I had to report to the police every week, Saturday afternoons. I did that for a while. The police sergeant, after about three or four months, he said to me, 'What do you keep coming here for?' 'Conditions of my release,' I said. He said, 'Don't bother about it,' so I never bothered any more.[2]

By 1945, the Isle of Man had closed its internment camps and returned the quarters to their peacetime purpose of welcoming holidaymakers and tourists.

Many years later Albert was interviewed about his experience of internment during the Second World War. He said:

> They [LBC Radio] said, 'Don't you feel bitter about the way you've been treated?' 'No,' I said, 'I sort of expected

it, 'cos I knew this sort of thing goes on, but what I did not like was the six months I spent in prison, now that I considered very unfair. I mean I wasn't a criminal, I'd done nothing wrong and yet I was put in prison like that, subject to all the rigours of prison life, I mean locked up some days 23 hours a day, other days they let you out you know for a bit longer things like that.' That was the only thing I didn't like, once I got to internment camps, it was a pleasure.[3]

The British government never offered compensation for the four years Albert was interned, so Albert got in touch with the Home Office to see if he could apply instead:

I wrote to the Home Office and I said I'd like to ask for something because you know I lost four years of my life for no reason at all. How could I go about it? 'What were you interned under?' Defence Regulation 18B. 'Oh,' he said, 'all those records have been burnt'. I said if I gave you my name wouldn't that help? 'No. All burnt.'[4]

Although he had served time as a prisoner, Albert did not have a criminal record because he was an unconvicted prisoner. He eventually married, had children and lived in North London.

Joe Pieri was released from internment in November 1943. As the war was still going on, the ship in which Joe left Canada crossed the Atlantic in convoy. He was initially taken to the Isle of Man, where he stayed for a few months. Eventually his mother and father found him employment of national importance working on a farm near Glasgow, and Joe was allowed to return:

> I always remember the worst experience I had in my three years of internment was the day I was released from the Isle of Man. I was given a train ticket, I was given a few shillings in my pocket, I was put on a ferry and told, 'Get the train and go home.' I arrived at Liverpool station and I must have looked like a scrubbed convict or something; they gave me clothes because I had no clothes of my own. I was stood at the station platform with British soldiers all over the place. The train came in to go to Glasgow; I got into a compartment full of soldiers, men and women going home on leave, and I'm the only civilian there. They didn't know I was Italian because I spoke just as good English or Scots as they did ... and they were trying to bring me into their conversation. Here I am

sitting, I'm an ex-enemy alien, what would these people think if they knew I had been a prisoner for three years? So I pretended to go to sleep and eventually I did go to sleep. It's as though there's a spring inside you that knots up and helps you cope with the psychology of being a prisoner ... then you're released, the spring breaks and you're free, but you're still a prisoner because the people around you are the people that put you in behind barbed wire. So you're alone, isolated, you know ... so [for] an internee, the imprisonment doesn't stop at the moment of release from behind barbed wire, psychologically it goes on for a long time after that.[5]

Eventually Joe returned home to the flat above the fish and chip shop in Renfrew Street, Glasgow. The family-run business had been kept open by Joe's mother and father so that their sons would have a job to return to after the war, Joe from internment and his brother from the British army. Returning to work behind the counter of the shop that he had seen smashed to pieces several years before was not easy for Joe:

I had to go and stand behind the counter and serve the very people that considered me an enemy alien. I had to ease myself into it; you know five minutes at a time, ten minutes at a time. I was completely fully integrated into the society into which I lived at the time and suddenly something happens and you're told by that society you're an enemy alien. You're not given a chance to talk to anybody and explain. You're grabbed, you're put in prison cell, from a prison cell you're put in a camp, from a camp you're put in a ship, from a ship you're put in another camp, and whether you like it or not that's what they considered me.[6]

Joe remained in Scotland, and later married a Scottish woman and started a family. He continued working in the catering industry until his retirement. Later he became the author of several books including *Isle of the Displaced*, about his experiences of internment during the Second World War.

Of the Italians who had been interned in Australia, most returned in 1946. When Rando Bertoia went home to Glasgow in that year, he found that the xenophobia that was directed towards Italians when Italy declared war had disappeared:

When I came back there was nobody against me or anything, and even my family, my father, there was nobody against, nothing at all, no animosity no anything. Actually some of the people said, 'Oh we're very sorry Italy declared war against us.' They were sorry but what can you do?[7]

Rando's father had been interned for around eight months on the Isle of Man. The company he worked for, Toffolo Jackson, a *terrazo* firm, used their influence to obtain his release for his knowledge in materials such as concrete. Rando was employed in the same trade but used the opportunity to start afresh. He married and had children, and along with his brother opened a shop in South Glasgow called Victoria Watchmakers, where he worked until he retired in 2007 at the age of 87.

Angelo Albericci returned to Britain in 1945. He could not get his old job back in Leeds or find work in any of the LMS railway hotels. He was eventually offered a job at the Savoy Hotel in London, where the restaurant manager, believed to be a man by the surname of Santarelli, had survived the *Arandora Star* and was interned in Australia along with Angelo. Angelo lodged in Kennington, in London, while his family stayed in Leeds until he was able to buy a house in London and the family eventually joined him.

In a few cases, men had been deported single but returned to Britain married. In the spring of 1944 Vittorio Tolaini was released and was found work in a hotel in Melbourne. He met an Italian girl called Noemi and married on 8 March 1945. At the end of 1946 they returned together to London, where they later had two sons. Noemi and Vittorio set up a restaurant with Nicky Cua (another survivor from the *Arandora Star* who had been sent to Australia) and retired around 1982. He wrote his story of internment in an unpublished manuscript called 'Voyage of an Alien', which is now at the Imperial War Museum in London.

Men who returned from camps in Canada, Australia and the Isle of Man slowly began to adjust to their newfound freedom. Women and children became accustomed to having men back in their lives as husbands and fathers. For all the heartache and hardship that the families endured, from those who experienced internment to those who had their male relatives interned, they were the fortunate ones: they returned with their lives and could build a future together as families at home in Britain. By far the biggest impact internment had was on the families of the 446 Italians who perished on 2 July 1940 when the *Arandora Star* was torpedoed.

16

Commemoration

It was several years before a version of the events of 2 July 1940, other than those in the newspapers and the telegram through the post, would be given to the families of the men lost on the *Arandora Star*. The several hundred men who returned from Australia and had been away the longest were also survivors of the sinking of the *Arandora Star* and eyewitnesses to the events leading up to, during and after the disaster. These survivors began to tell their story to family and friends, and explained how it was that they had survived the tragedy while others in the family had not.

Liliana Cortesio lost her father Giovanni, but her uncle, Vittorio Sartor, survived and was taken to Australia and later returned to London. Liliana, who was a young girl at the time, recalls that he would tell the story when the family met:

> We had the [family] lunch and he [Vittorio] was sitting at the head of the table and always talked about the *Arandora Star*. Thinking later on, well he must just have

to get it out of his system but he didn't tell us everything, because what I know now [2006] he didn't tell half. Perhaps he did that out of respect for my mother.[1]

Uberto Limentani, who had returned to the BBC, would later recount the story to his family too. His son Rupert said:

> For my brothers and me it obviously was a story with a happy ending because otherwise he wouldn't have been there to tell it. It wasn't a story that sort of shocked us or took our breath away. While we were children it seemed just like an episode of family folklore because it was something that nobody else had ever heard of and so there was no point in telling it to other people because nobody in England or Italy would have known what we were talking about if we had recounted it.[2]

Those who had lost fathers and other relatives in the disaster had only these few survivors' stories, along with the descriptions offered by the newspapers, to help them try to piece together what had happened to their loved ones. The newspapers had reported that the reason so many men died was that infighting between Italian and German internees had hindered the British rescue effort. Italian survivors spoke of how they had managed to survive: some by getting into a lifeboat, others by climbing down rope ladders or diving into the sea and swimming away on a piece of debris. However, they also spoke of how hundreds of the internees had died either injured in the initial blast by the torpedo, or unable to get to a lifeboat, being hampered by barbed wire entanglements, or trapped in their quarters below the water line, drowned because they didn't know how to swim, or dragged into the sea by barbed wire barricades. These reasons were very different from the infighting reported in the papers at the time. Eye-witness observations countered the report in the newspaper. Harold Finney, a guard on the *Arandora Star*, said: 'I never saw any of that [fighting].'[3] Rando Bertoia said: 'There was no fighting just people looking after themselves but no fighting.'[4] The panic described in the article was contradicted by Major G. A. I. Dury, a Liaison Officer on the *Arandora Star,* who stated: 'There was little or no panic among the internees.'[5]

An enquiry into the large loss of life was never conducted, and remarkably, even after the disaster, the deportations of internees continued with the *Ettrick* and the *Dunera*, sailing in circumstances similar to those of the *Arandora Star*. Joe Pieri said that if the *Ettrick* had been torpedoed, they would have all 'drowned like rats in a trap'.[6] The *Dunera* sailed to Australia in similar conditions and was twice torpedoed: 'We were torpedoed again,' said Rando Bertoia, who had travelled in a hold on the *Dunera*; 'two torpedoes were fired at us by our "allies".'[7] Luckily, the U-boat captain was not a crack shot like Günther Prien in U-47, and both torpedoes missed the ship.

Internment and the *Arandora Star* disaster had a deep and lasting impact on the families of the victims, but also on the police officers and Special Branch detectives who had carried out the arrests in June 1940. Used to arresting people on a charge, the officers were given by the Home Office the power to arrest without charge under the Aliens Act.

Robert Mark, at the time a young Special Branch officer who later became Commissioner of the Metropolitan Police, had arrested a man called Ernani Landucci. On the day of the arrest, Mark and a colleague named Pierpoint arrived at Landucci's home in Manchester. Landucci, a waiter at a Manchester hotel where he had worked for around 30 years, had a British-born daughter. Due to the blackout it is likely that Mark and Pierpoint arrested him in darkness and, given that the arrest was carried out at Landucci's house, in front of his wife and the child. Mark and Pierpoint questioned Landucci on his membership of the *fascio*, and he replied that he was a member because he owned a piece of land in southern Italy that he had to pay tax on to the Italian Consul General, and being a member of the party helped speed up the process. This was all the evidence against Landucci. Mark believed Landucci's story and assured him that he would report his findings to his superiors and recommend release, which he did the following day. Landucci was never released and died in the *Arandora Star* disaster. Landucci's death had a profound impact on Mark's career and was an episode that stayed with him until his retirement.

The sense of injustice that was felt by Mark towards the death of Landucci in such tragic circumstances could also have been applied to the fates of several hundred

Italian victims with membership or association with the *fasci* in Britain. 'My parents never belonged to the party,' said Graziella, whose father was a musician and taught violin at the Casa del Littorio.[8] According to Graziella, most of the Italians who went to the Littorio were nominal members who wanted to take advantage of the cultural activities, be among other Italians in a safe environment and express patriotism rather than fascist ideology.

Rita Pezzani's parents also used to go to the Littorio in London. Rita's father, Nello Cardosi, who had rejected Count Bastianini's offer of repatriation to Italy, had been arrested and deported on the *Arandora Star*. He had survived the sinking of the ship and had been on a raft along with an interned Italian priest and Armando Bertuzzi, manager of the RAC club. Nello's younger brother, Valesco, was also on the *Arandora Star* and Nello decided to leave the raft and search for his brother. Although a strong swimmer, he had a history of suffering from pleurisy. Both Nello and Valesco were later declared missing presumed drowned. Far from being a 'dangerous character', in 1933 Nello was awarded a cheque for five guineas by Lloyds

Bank Limited for his public-spirited action on the occasion of an attempted robbery at the Stepney branch.

Peter Tarchetti was lost in the disaster, but rather than appearing on the list of Italians, as his surname would suggest, he appeared on the list of the British military guard as he was serving as a rifleman in the 9th Battalion Cameronians (Scottish Rifles) while on the *Arandora Star*. The death of Peter Tarchetti, the son of an Italian immigrant, drafted by the British government and lost at sea guarding Italian enemy aliens, highlights the futility of the internment and deportation of so-called enemy aliens.

A name that appears on the list of crew members missing was that of Rocco Sinacola, aged 23, from London. He was not an internee or a military guard but was working as a greaser on the *Arandora Star*. His father and mother were Ferdinand and Maria Sinacola of Vauxhall. It is unclear whether the parents were Italian and whether Ferdinand was interned, but the surname is of Italian origin.

With the capitulation of Italy in 1943, the Italian war effort against Britain came to an end, but the stigma of Italian association with the war continued. Many first-generation Italians, born in Italy but raised in Britain, and second-generation Italians concealed their Italian identities and anglicised their names, refusing to speak or learn Italian, and distancing their association with the country. Many internalised their feelings about the *Arandora Star* tragedy and remained silent about it.

Remembrance

On 21 March 1941 a Solemn Requiem Mass for Father
Fracassi was given at St Albans Church in Ancoats,
Manchester. Father Fracassi had been parish priest at St.
Albans, where most of the city's Italian population
attended. He had been interned and deported on the
Arandora Star and was lost in the disaster. In a statement,
the Bishop of Salford, Dr Henry Vincent Marshall, explained
how Cardinal Hinsley had tried to secure the release of
Father Fracassi and have him sent home to Italy. He went
on:

> [I] knew him very well and knew also that he was
> violently opposed to his country's entering the war
> against this country, and he would never listen in to
> Italian broadcasts because of the propaganda that was
> being sent out. [He] lived in extreme poverty, and on one
> occasion made the mistake of renting his club to a
> political party. But after all, the letting of the club was no
> worse than letting of the Free Trade Hall to political

bodies and other organisations I have heard of. I want to say that he was loyal to this country and he was in no way whatsoever connected with anybody working to harm this country. He was not by any means an enemy of Great Britain.[1]

The Home Office were responsible for the instructions given to the police regarding the internment of aliens. All the instructions issued made it clear that the invalid and the infirm were not to be interned. Father Fracassi was an invalid but deported.

The trauma of the Italian community could not be internalised forever, and their pain was expressed in remembrance two decades later. On 4 November 1960 a memorial was unveiled at St Peter's Italian Church in Clerkenwell, London. It was funded by donations from the Italian community in London and was mounted on the outer wall. The writing is in Italian, and translated it reads: 'In memory of those lost in the sinking of the *Arandora Star* 2 July 1940 ... a memory that lives on in the hearts of the relatives, survivors and the Italian colony.'[2]

In central and northern Italy, where most of the men came from, remembrance of the tragedy is marked by several plaques and chapels where relatives of the dead can pay their respects. The small town of Bardi, built on top of a hill in Emilia-Romagna, lost 48 men in the disaster. Most had been living in Wales at the time of the war. A chapel to the town's victims is located in the cemetery, and each year a memorial service is held, where people can write tributes in a book of remembrance. There is also a road in the town called Via Arandora Star.

In Borgotaro, another town in Emilia-Romagna, there is also a road called Via Arandora Star, and one called Via Colonsay. Borgotaro lost six men on the *Arandora Star*, and one of these was Giuseppe Del Grosso, whose body washed ashore on the Island of Colonsay where he was buried at Leum a' Brhair. He was later reinterred in Glasgow Roman Catholic Cemetery. In a show of gratitude to the Island, Borgotaro named this road to commemorate the links between the two places and to thank the people of Colonsay. A cairn on the island marks the spot where Giuseppe Del Grosso was buried. A memorial plaque is located nearby to his memory and that of all those who lost their lives on the *Arandora Star*.

In Britain, apart from the Italian-funded memorial at St Peter's Church in Clerkenwell, few memorials existed to commemorate the loss of the victims. However, on 2 July 2008, 68 years after the sinking of the ship, a service at Liverpool's Parish church of Our Lady and St Nicholas was held and Diplomatic representatives from Italy and Germany joined several hundred relatives and friends of the dead. Present were Frank Longinotti, Rita Pezzani and Graziella Feraboli, who lost their fathers in the disaster; Evan Morgan Jones (89), formerly of the Welsh regiment and a guard on the *Arandora Star*, and Rando Bertoia, formerly an Italian internee and a survivor of the disaster, from Glasgow, also attended. The Italian Ambassador unveiled a bronze plaque to honour the men who died.

It is now possible for relatives to go and pay their respects at Liverpool, from where the ship set sail. A plaque at Pier Head has, at top centre, the European union flag as a backdrop; the flag of the Blue Star Line, owners of the *Arandora Star*, is in the middle within a ship's steering wheel with the name of the *Arandora Star* inside it. The plaque reads: 'In memory of those who sailed from Liverpool on SS *Arandora Star* and who tragically lost their lives when the ship was sunk by torpedo 75 Miles North West of Donegal on 2 July 1940. Of 1,673 people aboard, over 800 mainly non-combatants drowned.' (Lists of men who perished in the disaster are included in the appendix of this book.)

The commemorative day was organised by Nunzia Bertali, Italian honorary consul for Liverpool District, Councillor Flo Clucas, and Graham Boxer of Liverpool City Council. The plaque was designed by Fred O'Brien, of Northern Design Unit. After a commemorative concert and readings at Merseyside Maritime Museum, wreaths were cast into the river from a Mersey ferry.

Graziella and her mother had barely a chance to mourn their loss at the time as a few weeks later the Blitz arrived and they concentrated their efforts on surviving the bombings in London that were to last for 57 consecutive nights. Having been evacuated to Portsmouth with her school in September 1939, Graziella never had a chance to say goodbye to her father. After his arrest, she returned to London to be with her mother. She remembered:

> The morning of 2 July [1940], I had left my bedroom rushed into my mother's room, crying really weeping and

saying I'm never going to see my father again, I'm never going to see my father again, and I had no reason to say that. And my mother was very cross with me and she said, 'Stop it! Don't say such stupid things.' It was about 6.30 in the morning that I ran into my mother's room crying and I have the feeling that there was telepathy between my father and myself in the moment that he was drowning, that he thought of his family, and the thought was transmitted and I have never forgotten that moment.[3]

Graziella and her mother lived without news of Ettore until weeks after his arrest, when they received a letter from him addressed from Wharf Mills. They wrote back, but their letter never reached him. His journey to Liverpool and eventually onto the *Arandora Star*, along with several hundred other men, was made at a greater speed than the letter's journey to the camp. 'He died not knowing what happened to us and we lived not knowing what happened to him, until that fatal day at Hobart House [Brazilian Embassy],'[4] said Graziella.

For Graziella and relatives of those missing presumed drowned present in Liverpool 68 years later, who were children at the time, the recognition of the disaster and the unveiling of the plaque at Liverpool dock, where the *Arandora Star* set sail, provided some form of closure after such a long wait and such a long silence.

End Note

The British government was not the only one to intern
foreign nationals belonging to enemy countries during the
Second World War. The United States government also
used this defence measure to counter the potential threat of
an enemy within. The US entered the conflict after the
Japanese attack on the US naval base at Pearl Harbor on 7
December 1941, declaring war on Japan. Subsequently
Germany and Italy declared war on the US. In 1942 there
were around 695,000 Italian enemy aliens in the US. Some
1,880 were taken into custody and detained under wartime
restrictions by the Department of Justice, using the Aliens
and Sedition Act. This was applied in the main to Italian
nationals, not US citizens or long-term US residents. Around
112,000 Japanese were evacuated from the West Coast of
the United States and interned in the interior of the country
after US President Franklin D. Roosevelt signed Executive
Order 9066 on 19 February 1942. Over 60 per cent were US
citizens.

In 2001 the US Attorney General carried out a
review of the treatment of Italians by the Department of

Justice and its enforcement of the Alien and Sedition Act. In 2010 the California Legislature passed a resolution apologising for US mistreatment of Italians resident during the Second World War.

In 1980 the US government held an investigation into the evacuation of Japanese residents and found that it was unjustified and that there was little evidence of Japanese disloyalty. In response, on 10 August 1988 the Civil Liberties Act provided $1.65 billion in restitution to 82,000 people of Japanese ancestry who endured unnecessary suffering during the Second World War. Each received $20,000, along with a letter of apology from the then President, Ronald Reagan. Also $5 million was authorised to fund education programmes on the wartime evacuation and relocation. The author is not aware of a similar initiative by the British government to date with regard to its role in interning enemy aliens.

Appendix I

List of Italian provincial abbreviations

(Ag) Agrigento, Sicilia

(Al) Alessandria, Piemonte

(An) Ancona, Marche

(Ao) Aosta, Valle d' Aosta

(Ar) Arezzo, Toscana

(Ap) Ascoli Piceno, Marche

(At) Asti, Piemonte

(Av) Avellino, Campania

(Ba) Bari, Puglia

(Bl) Belluno, Veneto

(Bn) Benevento, Campania

(Bg) Bergamo, Lombardia

(Bo) Bologna, Emilia-Romagna

(Bz) Bolzano, Trentino Alto Adige

(Bg) Brescia, Lombardia

(Br) Brindisi, Puglia

(Ca) Cagliari, Sardegna

(Cl) Caltanissetta, Sicilia

(Cb) Campobasso, Molise

(Ce) Caserta, Campania

(Ct) Catania, Sicilia

(Cz) Catanzaro, Calabria

(Ch) Chieti, Abruzzo

(Co) Como, Lombardia

(Cs) Cosenza, Calabria

(Cr) Cremona, Lombardia

(Cn) Cuneo, Piemonte

(En) Enna, Sicilia

(Fe) Ferrara, Emilia-Romagna

(Fi) Firenze, Toscana

(Fg) Foggia, Puglia

(Fo) Forli, Emilia-Romagna

(Fr) Frosinone, Lazio

(Ge) Genova, Liguria

(Go) Gorizia, Friuli-Venezia Giulia

(Gr) Grosseto, Toscana

(Im) Imperia, Liguria

(Is) Isernia, Molise

(Aq) L'Aquila, Abruzzo

(Sp) La Spezia, Liguria

(Lt) Latina, Lazio

(Le) Lecce, Puglia

(Li) Livorno, Toscana

(Lu) Lucca, Toscana

(Mc) Macerata, Marche

(Mn) Mantova, Lombardia

(Ms) Massa-Carrara, Toscana

(Mt)Matera,Basilicata

(Me) Messina, Sicilia

(Mi) Milano, Lombardia

(Mo) Modena, Emilia-Romagna

(Na) Napoli, Campania

(No) Novara, Piemonte

(Nu) Nuoro, Sardegna

(Or) Oristano, Sardegna

(Pd) Padova, Veneto

(Pa) Palermo, Sicilia

(Pr) Parma, Emilia-Romagna

(Pv) Pavia, Lombardia

(Pg) Perugia, Umbria

(Ps) Pesaro, Marche

(Pe) Pescara, Abruzzo

(Pc) Piacenza, Emilia-Romagna

(Pi) Pisa, Toscana

(Pt) Pistoia, Toscana

(Pn) Pordenone, Friuli-Venezia Gulia

(Pz) Potenza, Basilicata

(Rg) Ragusa, Sicilia

(Ra) Ravenna, Emilia-Romagna

(Rc) Reggio Calabria, Calabria

(Re) Reggio Emilia, Emilia Romagna

(Ri) Rieti, Lazio

(Roma) Roma, Lazio

(Ro) Rovigo, Veneto

(Sa) Salerno, Campania

(Ss) Sassari, Sardegna

(Sv) Savona, Liguria

(Si) Siena, Toscana

(Sr) Siracusa, Sicilia

(So) Sondrio, Lombardia

(Ta) Taranto, Puglia

(Te) Teramo, Abruzzo

(Tr) Terni, Umbria

(To) Torino, Piemonte

(Tp) Trapani, Sicilia

(Tn) Trento, Trentino Alto Adige

(Tv) Treviso, Veneto

(Ts) Trieste, Friuli-Venezia Giulia

(Ud) Udine, Friuli-Venezia Giulia

(Va) Varese, Lombardia

(Ve) Venezia, Veneto

(Vc) Vercelli, Piemonte

(Vr) Verona, Veneto

(Vi) Vicenza, Veneto

(Vt) Viterbo, Lazio

Courtesy of Terri Colpi

Appendix II

Arandora Star: Missing person list Italians

Surname and Christian name, DOB, Birth Place, Last Place of Residence

1. Abrardo, Eraldo Giuseppe, 15.04.1892, Fubine (AL) London E
2. Abruzzese, Giocondino, 26.08.1875, Filignano (IS), Glasgow S
3. Adami, Paolo, 29.05.1909, Trieste (TS), London E
4. Affaticati, Riccardo, 02.08.1893, Caorso (PC) London E
5. Aglieri, Mario, 21.05.1887, Milano (MI), London E
6. Agostini, Oliviero, 29.04.1904, Barga (LU), Glasgow S
7. Albertella, Giovanni, 13.01.1893, Cannero (NO) Lancaster E
8. Albertelli, Carlo, 30.05.1899, Morfasso (PC), Pontypridd W
9. Alberti, Humbert, 28.10.1881, Barga (LU), Manchester E
10. Albertini, Constante, 08.04.1885, Milano (MI), London E
11. Allera, Lorenzo, 17.09.1900, Ivrea (TO), London E
12. Alliata, Publio, 19.08.1884, Roma ROMA, London E
13. Amodeo, Tullio Edouard, 29.07.1882, Roma, ROMA, London, E
14. Andreassi, Giuseppe, 19.03.1880, San Demetrignei (CS), London E
15. Angella, Emilio, 02.07.1896, Pontremoli (MS), Bolton, E
16. Angiolini, Domenico Giuseppe, 15.03.1900, Genova (GE), Glasgow S
17. Aniballi, Giuseppe, 06.09.1896, Amatrice (RI), London E
18. Antoniazzi, Bartolomeo, 20.01.1908, Bardi (PR), Newtown W
19. Anzani, Decio, 10.07.1882, Forli (FO), London E
20. Arnoldi, Ercole, 03.09.1910, Taleggio (BG), London E
21. Avella, Alfonso, 04.07.1889, Tirreni (PI), Glasgow S
22. Avignone, Giovanni, 02.05.1887, Port St Martin, London E
23. Avignone-Rossa, Italo, 12.10.1907, Bollengo (TO) London E
24. Avondoglio, Fortunato, 03.07.1888, Chiaversano (TO), London, E
25. Azario, Efisio Remo Vitale, 18.06.1885, Mosso, Santa Maria (VC) London E
26. Babini, Lorenzo, 16.11.1885, Lugo ?, London E
27. Baccanello, Marco, 03.04.1898, Venezia (VE), Harpenden E

28. Bagatta, Angelo, 26.03.1883, S. Columbano Al Lambro (MI), London E
29. Baldieri, Armando, 26.06.1912, Roma ROMA, London E
30. Ballerini, Roberto, 02.05.1895, Galluzzo ?, London E
31. Banino, Luigi, 21.08.1904, Cerione (VC), London E
32. Barone Francesco, 13.09.1889, San Paolo -, London E
33. Baroni, Alessandro, 11.08.1880, Milano (MI) London E
34. Basilico, Cesare, 15.06.1885, Cavonno Milanese (MI), London E
35. Basini, Bartolomeo, 12.10.1908, Bardi (PR), Tre Herbert W
36. Battistini, Umberto, 23.05.1899, Stazzema (LU), Ayr S
37. Bava, Claudio, 20.03.1887, Montechiaro D'Asti (AT), Gateshead E
38. Belli, Antonio, 08.11.1885, Bardi (PR), Maestag W
39. Bellini, Pietro, 08.07.1878, Morfasso (PC), London E
40. Belmonte, Gaetano, 16.09.1876, Cassino (FR), Edinburgh S
41. Belotti, Leone, 17.02.1904, Bergamo (BG), West Wickham E
42. Beltrami, Alessandro, 20.12.1874, Egypt -, Glasgow S
43. Beltrami, Leandro, 11.08.1890, Massemino (SV) Middlesbrough E
44. Benigna, Pietro, 01.11.1904, Chiuduno (BG), Leicester E
45. Benini, Giuseppe, 14.03.1881, Bologna (BO), London E
46. Berigliano, Antonio, 17.01.1899, Dorzano (VC), London E
47. Berni, Attilio, 10.05.1899, Bardi (PR), Weston-Sp-Mare E
48. Berra, Claudio Giacomo, 16.07.1890, S. Quirico (VI), London E
49. Bersani, Carlo, 07.06.1889, Sarmato (PC), London E
50. Bertin, Antonio, 11.10.1901, Sequals (PN), London E
51. Bertoia, Luigi, 04.06.1921, Montereale (PN), Middlesbrough E
52. Bertolini, Vincenzo Silvio, 14.06.1876, Barga (LU), Glasgow S
53. Bertoncini, Pietro, 24.11.1887, Camporgiano (LU), London E
54. Bertucci, Siro Celestino, 01.02.1885, Vercelli (VC), London E
55. Beschizza, Anselmo, 29.04.1878, Bratto (MS), London E
56. Beschizza, Raffaele, 12.11.1910, Pontremoli (MS), London E
57. Biagi, Luigi, 16.04.1898, Gallicano (LU), Ayr S
58. Biagioni, Ferdinando, 06.07.1895, Barga (LU), Glasgow S
59. Biagioni, Francesco, 06.03.1897, Castelnuovo G. (LU), Rothesay S
60. Biagioni, Umberto, 23.04.1878, Castelnuovo G. (LU), Glasgow S
61. Biagiotti, Carlo, 04.06.1877, Pistoia (PT), Glasgow S

62. Biagiotti, Nello, 25.02.1893, Pistoia (PT), Glasgow S
63. Bich, Clement Daniele, 21.12.1887, Valtournenche (AO), Thames Ditton E
64. Bigi, Mansneto, 08.08.1885, Gualteri (RE), Highcliffe on Sea E
65. Bigogna, Giuseppe, 10.11.1900, Acqui ?, London E
66. Bissolotti, Carlo, 24.11.1900, Soresina (CR), London E
67. Boccassini, Attilio, 10.10.1890, Barletta (BA), London E
68. Bombelli, Mario, 18.09.1885, Roma ROMA, Cardiff W
69. Bonaldi, Andrea Luigi, 18.06.1898, Songavazzo (BG), London E
70. Bonati, Alfonso, 02.07.1893, Riccò Del Golfo (SP), Glasgow S
71. Bonetti, Giovanni, 23.02.1881, Lograto (BS), Southampton E
72. Bongiovanni, Pietro, 20.04.1891, Savona (SV), London E
73. Bono, Luigi, 24.01.1890, Arona (NO), London E
74. Borgo, Carlo, 03.04.1897, Casatisma (PV), London E
75. Borrelli, Federico, 12.12.1887, Schiava ?, London E
76. Borsumato, Alessandro, 02.11.1896, Cassino (FR), Middlesbrough E
77. Boscasso, Magno, 02.06.1881, Montechiaro D'Asti (AT), London E
78. Bragoli, Pietro, 23.05.1880, Morfasso (PC), London E
79. Bragoni, Ilario, 14.01.1897, Villa Franca (FO), London E
80. Bravo, Francesco, 30.03.1892, Bollengo (TO), London E
81. Breglia, Salvatore Gaetano, 13.07.1895, Napoli (NA), Cambridge E
82. Broggi, Vittorio, 08.07.1902, Gavirate (VA), London E
83. Brugnoni, Mario Maximilian, 25.08.1904, Paris -, London E
84. Bucchioni, Lorenzo, 23.03.1899, Pontremoli (MS), London E
85. Caldera, Carlo, 21.01.1896, Alice Castello (VC), London E
86. Calderan, Emilio, 06.09.1900, Torino (TO), London E
87. Callegari, Luigi, 27.03.1899, Torino (TO), London E
88. Camillo, Giuseppe, 04.10.1882, S. Cosmo (LT), Glasgow S
89. Camozzi, Cesare, 02.11.1891, Iseo (BR), Manchester E
90. Capella, Giuseppe, 13.04.1885, Borgotaro (PR), London E
91. Capitelli, Carlo, 28.04.1899, Borgotaro (PR), London E
92 Capitelli, Eduardo, 18.07.1882, Albareto (PR), London E
93. Cardani, Carlo, 28.04.1886, Sesto Calende (VA), London E
94. Cardarelli, Quirino, 17.05.1889, Roma ROMA, London E

95. Cardellino, Giovanni, 18.12.1886, San Damiano (LT), London E
96. Cardosi, Nello, 17.02.1902, Brunswick -, London E
97. Cardosi, Valesco, 24.12.1910, Camporgiano (LU), London E
98. Carini, Francesco, 15.07.1893, Bardi (PR), Pontypridd W
99. Carini, Giuseppe, 21.05.1898, Bardi (PR), Ebbw Vale W
100. Carpanini, Giovanni, 05.01.1919, Bardi (PR), Britton Ferry W
101. Carpanini, Giuseppe, 17.07.1892, Bardi (PR), Cwmcarn W
102. Casali, Giuseppe, 03.08.1909, Morfasso (PC), London E
103. Castelli, Antonio, 18.10.1894, Bettola (PC), Aberdare E
104. Castellotti, Giovanni, 15.06.1899, Pontremoli (MS), London E
105. Cattini, Giacobbe Pietro, 01.06.1918, Bratto (MS), London E
106. Cattini, Pietro, 02.11.1881, Bratto (MS), London E
107. Cattolico, Mario Fedrico, 16.04.1891, Napoli (NA), Stanmore E
108. Cavaciutti, Pietro, 06.06.1893, Morfasso (PC), London E
109. Cavadini, Achille, 26.03.1891, Como (CO), London E
110. Cavalli, Giovanni, 04.02.1889, Bardi (PR), Neath W
111. Cavalli, Nicolas, 06.05.1892, Felizzano (AL), London E
112. Ceresa, Antonio, 20.06.1889, Bollengo (TO), London E
113. Ceresa, Eduardo, 29.05.1890, Bollengo (TO), Chorlton Medlock E
114. Ceresa, Stefano, 22.05.1900, Bollengo (TO), London E
115. Chiappa, Emilio Domenico, 16.09.1900, Bedonia (PR), Bridgend W
116. Chiappelli, Oraldo, 14.05.1920, Pistoia (PT), Glasgow S
117. Chiarcossi, Giovanni, 09.01.1875, Gradisca di Sedegliano (UD), London E
118. Chietti, Emilio Ottavio, 03.09.1886, Monte Folonico (SI), London E
119. Chiodi, Domenico, 29.10.1912, Braia (MS), London E
120. Ciampa, Salvatore, 07.02.1884, Messina (ME), London E
121. Ciarli, Vittorio, 31.07.1897, Quagneto (NA), Edinburgh S
122. Ciotti, Pasquale, 09.11.1890, Coseiago ?, London E
123. Cimorelli, Giovanni, 23.06.1875, Montaquila (IS), Edinburgh S
124. Cini, Armando, 09.06.1886, Cairo -, London E
125. Colella, Vincenzo, 25.04.1895, Viticuso (FR), London E
126. Coniola, Celeste, 06.04.1883, Pontari Genova (GE), Bradford E
127. Conti, Abramo, 04.09.1894, Venezia, (VE), London E
128. Conti, Guido, 26.12.1908, Bardi (PR), Newport W

129. Conti, Giuseppe, 19.03.1898, Bardi (PR), Treharris W
130. Copolla, Philip, 07.01.1895, Picinisco (FR), Edinburgh S
131. Coppola, Paolo, 05.09.1878, Picinisco (FR), Edinburgh S
132. Corrieri, Leonello Giuseppe, 16.10.1888, ??, Wallasey E
133. Cortesio, Giovanni, 13.01.1899, Savigliano (CN), London E
134. Cosomino, Giovanni, 03.05.1880, Barga (LU), Bellshill S
135. Costa, Diamante, 28.10.1882, Parma (PR), London E
136. Cristofoli, Domenico, 14.04.1905, Sequals (PN), Birmingham E
137. Cristofoli, Ettore, 12.09.1896, Sequals (PN), London E
138. Cristofoli, Renato, 10.02.1908, Autun (PN), London E
139. Crolla, Alfonso, 24.05.1888, Picinisco (FR), Edinburgh S
140. Crolla, Donato, 07.09.1880, Paris -, Edinburgh S
141. D'Ambrosio, Francesco, 02.12.1879, Picinisco (FR), Swansea W
142. D'Ambrosio, Silvestro, 30.12.1872, Picinisco (FR), Hamilton S
143. D'Annunzio, Antonio, 22.09.1905, Villa Latina (FR), Glasgow S
144. D'Inverno, Francesco, 17.04.1901, Villa Latina (FR), Ayr S
145. Da Prato, Silvio, 27.02.1878, Barga (LU), Glasgow S
146. Dalli, Pietro, 10.10.1893, ??, Ayr S
147. Danieli, Daniele, 23.03.1878, Monte di Malo (VI), ? -
148. De Angeli, Mario, 14.02.1906, Milano (MI), London E
149. De Gasperis, Carlo, 01.09.1906, Tivoli ROMA, London E
150. De Marco, Lorenzo, 05.02.1885, Picinisco (FR), Edinburgh S
151. De Marco, Pasquale, 10.04.1898, Caserta (CE), Glasgow S
152. De Rosa, Carlo, 11.02.1882, Napoli (NA), London E
153. Del Grosso, Giuseppe, 20.04.1889, Borgotaro (PR), Hamilton S
154. Delicato, Carmine, 17.02.1900, Atina (FR), Edinburgh S
155. Delzi, Carlo, 02.10.1913, Livorno (LI), London E
156. Di Ciacca, Aristide, 06.10.1920, Picinisco (FR), Glasgow S
157. Di Ciacca, Cesidio, 20.10.1891, Picinisco (FR), Cockenzie S
158. Di Cocco, Domenico, 04.06.1876, Velliterro ?, Manchester S
159. Di Luca, Pietro, 29.09.1873, Rochetta Al Volturno (IS), Glasgow S
160. Di Marco, Mariano, 24.11.1897, Cassino (FR), Hamilton S
161. Di Marco, Michele, 08.05.1890, Picinisco (FR), Swansea W
162. Di Vito, Giuseppe, 25.11.1874, Casalattico (FR), Crossgates S
163. Dottori, Argilio, 20.01.1882, Roma ROMA, Southampton E

164. Ermini, Armando, 28.08.1890, Chitta ?, London E
165. Falco, Celestino, 01.08.1891, Cuneo (CN), London E
166. Fantini, Guglielmo, 03.08.1889, Napoli (NA), Southampton E
167. Farnocchi, Francesco, 09.06.1906, Stazzema (LU), Glasgow S
168. Fellini, Ettore, 25.09.1888, Savignoia ?, London E
169. Felloni, Giulio, 25.03.1905, Parma (PR), Aberdeen S
170. Feraboli, Ettore Innocente, 25.02.1885, Pessina (CR), London E
171. Ferdenzi, Carlo, 12.06.1897, Vernasca (PC), London E
172. Ferdenzi, Giacomo, 16.03.1898, New York -, London E
173. Ferdenzi, Giovanni, 15.06.1879, Vernasca (PC), London E
174. Ferdenzi, Giovanni, 20.05.1884, Vernasca (PC), London E
175. Ferrari, Francesco, 19.08.1899, Zignano ?, Port Glasgow S
176. Ferrari, Guido, 01.09.1893, Valdena (PR), Kirkcaldy S
177. Ferrari, Luigi, 19.10.1907, Bettola (PC), Aberdare W
178. Ferrero, Bernardo, 14.09.1890, Montechiaro D'asti (AT), London E
179. Ferri, Fiorentino, 22.01.1886, Filignano (IS), Bellshill S
180. Ferri, Giovanni, 12.07.1884, Vernasca (PC), Hull E
181. Filippi, Mario, 15.03.1910, Castelnuovo G. (LU), Ayr S
182. Filippi, Simone, 26.10.1878, Pieve (LU), Ayr S
183. Finazzi, Anniballe, 19.01.1903, Trescore (GR), London E
184. Fiorini, Clement, 20.01.1888, Sora (FR), Manchester E
185. Fisanotti, Oreste, 09.08.1897, Mathi -, LondonE
186. Foglia, Claudio Silvo, 02.01.1891, Amatrice (RI), London E
187. Fontana, Giovanni, 18.07.1892, Frassinoro (MO), Carlisle E
188. Forte, Giuseppe, 03.01.1893, London -, Belfast NI
189. Forte, Onorio, 02.05.1880, Acre (FR), Chorlton Medlock E
190. Fossaluzza, Matteo, 25.11.1897, Cavasso (CR), London E
191. Fracassi, Gaetano, 18.04.1876, Pescarolo (CR), Manchester E
192. Franchi, Giacomo, 06.08.1896, Bardi (PR), New Tredegar W
193. Franciscono, Nicola, 03.12.1884, Alice Castello (VC), London E
194. Fratteroli, Giancinto, 06.09.1900, Picinisco (FR), Ayr S
195. Friggi, Egidio, 29.11.1886, Motta Visconti (MI), Southampton E
196. Frizzi, Carlo, 13.12.1873, Caserta (CE), Manchester E
197. Fulgoni, Giacomo, 10.07.1894, Grezzo Di Bardi (PR), Hirwaun W

198. Fulgoni, Giovanni, 04.07.1900, Grezzo Di Bardi (PR), Ponty Gwarth W
199. Fusco, Antonio, 26.08.1909, Casalattico (FR), Belfast NI
200. Fusco, Giovanni Antonio, 03.09.1877, Cassino (FR), Dundee S
201. Gabbini, Alfeo, 11.10.1897, Cannero (NO), London E
202. Gadeselli, Vincenzo, 15.09.1885, Bardi (PR), London E
203. Gagliardi, Battista, 28.02.1890, Milano (MI), London E
204. Gallo, Emilio, 20.11.1896, Belmonte (FR), Edinburgh S
205. Gargaro, Francesco, 25.05.1898, Picinisco (FR), Ayr S
206. Gazzi, Andrea, 02.08.1900, Bardi (PR), Gorsewinon W
207. Gazzi, Francesco, 12.01.1922, Bardi (PR), Pont Newydd W
208. Gazzi, Lino, 03.06.1881, Bardi (PR), Ferndale W
209. Gentile, Candido, 17.08.1894, Ventimiglia (IM), London E
210. Gerla, Giuseppe, 10.04.1893, Abbairati ?, London E
211. Ghiloni, Nello, 25.12.1909, Barga (LU), Glasgow S
212. Giannandrea, Vincenzo, 16.12.1910, Belmonte Castello (FR), Elgin S
213. Giannotti, Alfredo, 23.10.1885, Camporgiano (LU), London E
214. Giannotti, Ettore, 20.05.1910, Brescia (BS), London E
215. Giovanelli, Luigi, 24.04.1890, Bardi (PR), London E
216. Giraschi, Enrico, 22.02.1896, Pellegrino (PR), London E
217. Gonella, Francesco, 01.01.1885, Pontstaira ?, London E
218. Gonzaga, Luigi, 11.02.1924, Bedonia (PR), London E
219. Gorgone, Alfeo, 02.09.1909, Venezia (VE), London E
220. Gras, Davide, 03.02.1882, Bobbio Pelice (TO), London E
221. Greco, Domenico, 13.04.1885, Santo Padre (FR), Middlesbrough E
222. Greco, Tullio, 26.10.1897, Arpino (FR), Middlesbrough E
223. Grego, Anthony, 00.00.1891, Sora (FR), Greet E
224. Guarnori, Antonio, 17.02.1884, Novara (NO), London E
225. Guerri, Lino, 11.11.1914, Via Risasoli ?, London E
226. Gussoni, Ercole, 12.02.1902, Roma ROMA, London E
227. Gutkind, Curt Sigmar, 29.09.1896, Manheim -, London E
228. Iannetta, Ferdinando, 25.10.1889, Viticuso (FR), Edinburgh S
229. Iannetta, Orazio, 23.08.1901, Belmonte Castello (FR), Methil S
230. Iannetta, Vincenzo, 25.10.1902, Belmonte Castello (FR), Methil S

231. Iardella, Pietro, 05.07.1885, Pontremoli (MS), London E
232. Incerti, Rinaldi, 17.04.1884, Villa ??, London E
233. Jordaney, Giuseppe, 06.05.1888, Courmayeur (AO), London E
234. Landucci, Ernani, 29.09.1894, Firenze (FI), Chorlton Medlock E
235. Lanzi, Ugo, 01.04.1905, Milano (MI), London E
236. Lepora, Reino, 29.07.1897, Alice Castello (VC), London E
237. Longinotti, Giovanni, 17.05.1892, S.Maria Del Taro (PR), Heywood E
238. Lucantoni, Amedeo, 16.02.1897, Roma ROMA, Middlesbrough E
239. Lucchesi, Pietro, 26.01.1894, Castiglioni (LU), Prestwick S
240. Luise, Raffaele, 15.09.1905, Torre Del Greco (NA), London E
241. Lusardi, Tomasso Angelo, 29.05.1909, Blaengaru? (PN), London E
242. Lusardi, Vittorio, 23.07.1892, Bedonia (PR) Llanharen W
243. Maccariello, Elpidio, 16.05.1890, Casapulla (CE), London E
244. Maddalena, Marco Carlo, 16.12.1909, Fanna (PN), London E
245. Maggi, Cesare, 22.02.1887, Torino (TO), London E
246. Maiuri, Guido, 30.04.1877, Napoli (NA), London E
247. Mancini, Antonio, 03.08.1885, Atina (FR), Ayr S
248. Mancini, Domenico, 22.04.1881, Sessa (CE), Cholton Medlock E
249. Mancini, Umberto, 02.07.1891, Picinisco (FR), London E
250. Mancini, Vittorio, 19.04.1899, Picinisco (FR), London E
251. Manini, Cesare, 25.11.1903, Palazzolo (FI), London E
252. Marchesi, Charles Domenico, 17.07.1872, Codogno (MI), London E
253. Marchetto, Ugo, 18.04.1897, Venezia(VE), London E
254. Marello, Eugenio, 30.03.1893, Alfieri ?, London E
255. Marenghi, Giovanni, 23.04.1897, Bardi (PR), Pontypridd W
256. Marenghi, Luigi, 21.07.1893, Piacenza (PC), London E
257. Mariani, Amleto, 24.05.1887, Torino (TO), London E
258. Mariani, Pietro, 03.10.1921, Bardi (PR), London E
259. Marini, Luigi, 06.01.1912, Cuccaro (AL), London E
260. Mariotti, Fulgenzio, 23.09.1885, Costacciaro (PG), London E
261. Marre, Carlo, 03.08.1880, Borzonasca (GE), Manchester E
262. Marsella, Antonio, 15.10.1899, Casalattico (FR), Bonnybridge S
263. Marsella, Filippo, 07.04.1897, Casalattico (FR), Wishaw S
264. Marsella, Orlando, 22.08.1914, Glasgow -, Glasgow S

265. Martis, Orazio, 18.07.1883, Sassari (SS), New Malden E
266. Marzella, Antonio, 06.04.1899, Filignano (IS), Glasgow S
267. Massari, A, Unconfirmed
268. Mattei, Francesco, 13.10.1885, Sesso (RE), London E
269. Matteoda, Leopoldo, 30.07.1881, Saluzzo (CN), London E
270. Melaragni, Michelangelo, 18.03.1890, Cassino (FR), Manchester E
271. Menozzi, Gioacchino, 24.08.1894, Bardi (PR), London E
272. Meriggi, Mario, 17.08.1892, Portalbert -, London E
273. Merlo, Giuseppe, 29.03.1914, San Gallo (BG), Trealaw W
274. Meschi, Oscar, 16.07.1920, Fornoli (LU), Glasgow S
275. Meta, Pasqualino, 05.02.1899, Cassino (FR), Paisley S
276. Miele, Natalino, 25.12.1898, Cassino (FR), Edinburgh S
277. Miglio, Filippo Luigi, 19.05.1883, Trinito Cuneo (CN), London E
278. Milani, Luigi, 04.05.1890, Oggiono (CO), London E
279. Minetti, Giacomo, 11.07.1905, Bardi (PR), Neath S
280. Mittero, Antonio, 15.07.1908, Chieri (TO), Stalybridge E
281. Montagna, Giulio, 31.10.1888, Napoli (NA), London E
282. Monti, Giuseppe, 23.01.1889, Lacco Ameno (NA), Manchester E
283. Morelli, Luigi, 01.09.1892, Borgotaro (PR), London E
284. Moretti, Giovanni, 01.03.1900, Pardivarma (SP), Greenock S
285. Moruzzi, Ernesto, 12.08.1879, Bardi (PR), Neath W
286. Moruzzi, Peter, 31.05.1887, Bardi (PR), Neath W
287. Moruzzi, Pietro, 24.11.1917, Bardi (PR), London E
288. Moscardini, Santino, 02.01.1879, Barga (LU), Motherwell S
289. Musetti, Lorenzo, 25.02.1897, Buenos Aires -, London E
290. Musetti, Pietro, 31.01.1890, Pontremoli (MS), London E
291. Muzio, Enrico, 12.12.1892, Napoli (NA), London E
292. Nannini, Oreste, 28.05.1891, Pievepelago (MO), Edinburgh S
293. Nardone, Antonio, 20.10.1882, Cassino (FR), Middlesbrough E
294. Nichini, Giulio, 04.05.1896, Orta Novarese (NO), London E
295. Notafalchi, Lorenzo, 08.08.1885, Piacenza (PC), London E
296. Novelli, Vincenzo, 08.07.1893, Fubine (AL), London E
297. Olivelli, A, Unconfirmed
298. Operti, Egidio Ferrucio, 26.08.1890, Torino (TO), Southampton E
299. Orsi, Giuseppe, 22.06.1890, Albareto (PR), London E

300. Orsi, Pietro, 01.05.1888, Pontremoli (MS), London E
301. Ottolini, Giovanni, 21.07.1876, Lucca (LU), Birmingham E
302. Pacitti, Alfonso, 03.08.1887, Cerasuolo (IS), Glasgow S
303. Pacitti, Carmine, 03.06.1876, Filignano (IS), Carfin S
304. Pacitti, Gaetano, 10.12.1890, Villa Latina (FR), Edinburgh S
305. Pacitto, Gaetano Antonio, 19.10.1875, England -, Hull E
306. Palleschi, Nicola, 16.12.1884, Sesto Campano (IS), Glasgow S
307. Palumbo, Gioacchino, 21.03.1897, Minori (SA), London E
308. Paolozzi, Alfonso Rodolfo, 29.03.1901, Viticuso (FR), Edinburgh S
309. Papa, Pietro, 02.10.1909, S. Biagio (FR), Glasgow S
310. Pardini, Agostino, 09.09.1901, Capezzano (LU), Greenock S
311. Parmigiani, Giuseppe, 17.11.1889, Tourolo ?, London E
312. Pastecchi, Enrico, 06.03.1896, Roma ROMA, London E
313. Paulone, Amadeo, 24.03.1885, Scanno Aquila (AQ), Southampton E
314. Pellegrini, Domenico, 22.10.1894, Varsi (PR), London E
315. Pelosi, Paul, 23.03.1882, Picinisco (FR), Edinburgh S
316. Pelucco, Francesco, 12.04.1882, Quariento ?, London E
317. Perella, Luigi, 03.12.1893, Picinisco (FR), Edinburgh S
318. Peretti, Luigi, 01.10.1880, Agrano (NO), London E
319. Pettiglio, Carlo, 05.05.1878, Cassino (FR), Edinburgh S
320. Piancastelli, Annino, 26.07.1894, Busighella ?, London E
321. Picozzi, Carlo, 04.10.1889, Milano (MI), London E
322. Pieri, Alfredo, 08.11.1898, Lucca (LU), Carlisle E
323. Pieroni, Giuseppe, 31.01.1889, Pieve (MS), Ayr S
324. Piloni, Battista, 24.05.1897, Crema (CR), London E
325. Pinchera, Angelo Antonio, 31.08.1898, Cassino (FR), Glasgow S
326. Pinchiaroli, Luigi, 01.12.1894, Albareto (PR), Pontypridd W
327. Pino, Antonio Cesare, 18.10.1889, Lonigi (ME), London E
328. Piovano, Giacomo, 25.02.1892, Castelnuovo G. (LU), London E
329. Piscina, Giovanni, 16.05.1884, Parma (PR), London E
330. Plescia, Andrea, 16.01.1905, Palermo (PA), London E
331. Plescia, Baldassare, 01.01.1915, Palermo (PA), London E
332. Poli, Amedeo, 10.03.1896, Barga (LU), Glasgow S
333. Poli, Egisto, 17.11.1882, Colognara (LU), Glasgow S
334. Pollini, Manlio, 20.03.1883, Milano (MI), Southampton E

335. Pololi, Francesco, 06.03.1881, Toliggio ?, London E
336. Pompa, Ferdinando, 16.09.1876, Picinisco (FR), Swansea W
337. Pontone, Domenico, 13.08.1885, Cassino (FR), Hartlepool E
338. Pozzo, Giacinto, 20.04.1906, Viverone (VC), Whitton, Middx E
339. Prati, Carlo, 04.11.1877, Lugagnano (PC), Hull E
340. Previdi, Lodovico, 12.06.1895, Gropparello (PC), London E
341. Prister, Camillo Flavio, 28.06.1890, Gradisca (UD), Ilminster E
342. Puchoz, Marcello, 26.08.1896, Courmayeur (AO), London E
343. Pusinelli, Pietro, 03.04.1897, Naso (ME), London E
344. Quagliozzi, Angelo, 30.08.1881, Cassino (FR), Sheffield E
345. Quaranta, Domenico, 30.01.1883, Carbonara Napoli (NA), London E
346. Rabaiotti, Antonio, 20.10.1885, Bardi (PR), Newport W
347. Rabaiotti, Bartolomeo, 23.03.1881, Bardi (PR), Pontypridd W
348. Rabaiotti, Domenico, 12.02.1912, Bardi (PR), Ogmore Vale W
349. Rabaiotti, Francesco, 06.03.1894, Bardi (PR), Swansea W
350. Rabaiotti, Luigi, 11.12.1910, Bardi (PR), Swansea W
351. Raffetti, Carlo, 22.09.1901, Genova (GE), London E
352. Raggi, Luigi, 15.08.1880, Bardi (PR), London E
353. Ranaldi, Antonio, 16.01.1884, Arpino (FR), Middlesbrough E
354. Ravetto, Carlo, 09.01.1897, Alice Castello (VC), London E
355. Ravina, Cristoforo, 06.01.1882, Fulbrino ?, London E
356. Ravina, Giuseppe, 26.03.1884, Fubine (AL), London E
357. Razzuoli, Enrico, 15.12.1909, Stazzema (LU), Darvel S
358. Rea, Camillo, 06.10.1878, Arpino (FR), Middlesbrough E
359. Rea, Domenico, 07.01.1900, Arpino (FR), Middlesbrough E
360. Ricaldone, Allessandro Angelo, 03.12.1892, Fubine (AL), London E
361. Ricci, Lazzaro, 24.03.1891, Bardi (PR), Treharris W
362. Rinaldi, Giovanni, 31.03.1883, Artenes -, Leith S
363. Rivaldi, Patrocco, 18.01.1879, Cremona (CR), London E
364. Roccantonio, Francesco, 23.10.1875, Rocca D'Arce (FR), Peebles S
365. Rocchiccioli, Caesar, 06.12.1909, Barga (LU), Troon S
366. Roffo, Ernesto, 14.01.1896, Picinisco (FR), London E
367. Rosi, Guglielmo, 25.12.1893, Pontremoli (MS), London E
368. Rosi, Luigi, 16.12.1886, Grondola (MS), London E

369. Rossetto, Ferdinando, 19.06.1888, Bollengo (TO), London E
370. Rossi, Emilio, 08.09.1888, Viticuso (FR), Edinburgh S
371. Rossi, Eugenio, 17.10.1893, Paris -, Mountain Ash W
372. Rossi, Flavio, 15.06.1902, Bardi (PR), Port Glasgow S
373. Rossi Giovanni, 11.09.1923, Bardi (PR), Cardiff W
374. Rossi, Luigi, 14.08.1908, Bardi (PR), Swansea W
375. Rossi, Mario, 03.04.1889, Pisa (PI), London E
376. Rossi, Pietro, 23.12.1875, Viticuso (FR), Edinburgh S
377. Rossi, Vitale, 05.05.1898, Cavaglia (VC), London E
378. Rossotti, Carlo, 09.03.1899, Chieri Torino (TO), London E
379. Rota, Carlo, 20.03.1898, Giarole (AL), London E
380. Ruffoni, Giovanni Battista, 05.05.1885, Chignolo Verbano ?, London E
381. Ruocchio, Michele Andrew, 06.07.1908, ? ?, Larkhall S
382. Russo, Carmine, 24.07.1886, Cassino (FR), London E
383. Rustioni, Oreste, 09.07.1913, Milano (MI), London E
384. Sagramati, Vilfrido, 19.10.1910, Roma ROMA, London E
385. Sala, Emilio, 21.10.1912, Monza (MI), Luton E
386. Salsano, Luigi, 14.06.1921, Tramonti ?, London E
387. Sangalli, Gianetto, 12.07.1882, Milano (MI), London E
388. Santarello, Ferruccio, 17.12.1892, Venezia (VE), London E
389. Santi, S, Unconfirmed
390. Santini, Quinto, 29.07.1880, Pistoia (PT), Paisley S
391. Santuz, Antonio, 27.01.1884, Fanna (PN), Birmingham E
392. Sartori, Luigi, 14.04.1885, Morfasso (PC), London E
393. Scarabelli, Angelo Mario, 19.04.1892, S.Maria Della Verra (PV), London E
394. Sidoli, Giovanni, 17.08.1894, Bardi (PR), Glyncorrwg W
395. Sidoli, Luigi, 29.12.1882, Bardi (PR), London E
396. Siliprandi, Olimpio, 10.01.1883, Mantova (MN), Pettswood E
397. Silva, Luigi Antonio Mario, 11.11.1893, Via Anano ??, London E
398. Silverstrini, Giovanni, 24.04.1894, Verona (VR), London E
399. Simeone, Francesco, 27.01.1891, S. Vittorio Lazio (FR), London E
400. Sola, Carlo Frederico, 28.06.1882, Torino (TO), London E
401. Solari, Federico, 05.09.1914, Vernasca (PC), London E

402. Solari, Luigi, 24.04.1888, Bardi (PR), Neath W
403. Sottocornola, Edmondo, 02.04.1897, Gargallo (NO), London E
404. Sovrani, Giovanni Jean, 13.07.1882, Saludecio (FO), London E
405. Spacagna, Giuseppe, 09.03.1881, Cervaro (FR), Eastleigh E
406. Spagna, Antonio, 10.10.1894, Bardi (PR), Maesteg W
407. Spelta, Giuseppe, 07.03.1897, Milano (MI), Scarborough E
408. Speroni, Ermete, 27.11.1898, Milano (MI), Beckenham E
409. Stellon, Giovanni Maria, 14.09.1891, Fanna (PN), Newport W
410. Sterlini, Giuseppe, 31.05.1900, Bardi (PR), Wellington E
411. Sterlini, Marco, 17.10.1891, Bardi (PR), Tenby W
412. Storto, Giuseppe, 18.11.1900, Monferrato ?, London E
413. Stratta, Giacomo, 07.03.1894, Bollengo (TO), Croydon E
414. Strinati, Giovanni, 26.03.1880, Bardi (PR), Cwmaman W
415. Taffurelli, Giuseppe, 29.03.1892, Bettola (PC), Dowlais W
416. Taglione, Benedetto, 14.11.1883, Arpino (FR), London E
417. Tambini, Giovanni, 13.03.1899, Bardi (PR), Newport W
418. Tapparo, Luigi, 22.10.1898, Bollengo (TO), Edinburgh S
419. Tedesco, Raffaele, 03.09.1889, Mocera ?, Edinburgh S
420. Tempia, Giuseppe, 04.07.1896, Bollengo (TO), London E
421. Todisco, Antonio, 14.04.1893, Vallerotonda (FR), Redcar E
422. Togneri, Giuseppe, 19.03.1889, Barga (LU), Dunbar S
423. Tortolano, Giuseppe, 12.08.1880, Cassino (FR) Middlesbrough E
424. Tramontin, Riccardo, 24.11.1890, Cavasso Nuovo (PN), London E
425. Traversa, Italo Vittorio, 06.06.1918, Carisio (VC), London E
426. Trematore, Severino, 24.05.1895, Torre Maggiore (FO), London E
427. Trombetta, Pietro, 01.08.1892, Minori (SA), Chertsey E
428. Tuzi, Pasquale, 01.04.1898, Picinisco (FR), Edinburgh S
429. Vairo, Cesare, 26.07.1891, Milano (MI), London E
430. Valente, Adolf, 15.06.1900, Cervaro (FR), Edinburgh S
431. Valli, Giovanni, 20.09.1901, Novarro ?, London E
432. Valmaggia, Elio, 12.11.1896, Gemonio (VA), London E
433. Valvona, Enrico, 05.09.1885, Villa Latina (FR), London E
434. Vercelli, Emilio Giacomo, 01.08.1894, Mombercelli (AT), London E
435. Viccari, Antonio, 28.02.1890, Pontremoli (MS), London E
436. Viccari, Giulio, 31.05.1901, Pontremoli (MS), London E

437. Viccari, Pietro, 27.09.1889, SS. Cosmo e Damiano (FR), London E
438. Virno, Giovanni Battista, 07.10.1888, Cava Dei Tirreni (SA), London E
439. Zambellini, Luigi, 04.12.1887, Como (CO), London E
440. Zanelli, Etore, 03.11.1893, ? ?, Tonypandy W
441. Zanetti, Antonio, 09.07.1898, Varsi (PR), Swansea W
442. Zangiacomi, Italo, 16.04.1879, Verona (VR), London E
443. Zani, Guido, 30.11.1900, Pontremoli (MS), London E
444. Zanolli, Silvio, 09.04.1880, Monteforte ?, London E
445. Zavattoni, Etore, 19.08.1882, Villate (TO), London E
446. Zazzi, Luigi, 03.01.1895, Borgotaro (PR), London E

Courtesy of Terri Colpi

Appendix III

Arandora Star: Missing person list German

Surname and Christian name, D.O.B, Birth Place, Last place of residence

1. Baruch, Rolf, 05.05.1922, Hamburg, London E
2. Bergemann, Herman Emil, 24.09.1910, Altona, Tenby W
3. Bieber, Fritz, 10.02.1907, Berlin, Leeds E
4. Biermann, Wilhelm, 01.04.1906, Sallwarden, Oldenburg -
5. Birk, Karl, 11.05.1913, Freiendiez Unterlhan -
6. Blankenhorn, Bernhard, 23.06.1909, Mulhouse, Ipswich E
7. Bloch, Bertold, 05.07.1900, Randegg, Freetown -
8. Blumenthal, Alfons, 21.04.1907, Wiesbaden, Hackney E
9. Brandus-Nathan, Franz Israel, 07.06.1894, Magdeburg, Cardiff W
10. Breuer, Franz, 17.11.1885, Neuss, Hamburg -
11. Buhtz, Walter, 07.07.1909, Hermsdorf, Hermsdorf, Magdeburg –
12. Burfeind, Otto Jacob Heinrich, 09.01.1885, Altona, Blankensee Sueldurfer –
13. Dabel, Friedrich Wilhelm, 27.08.1911, Stralsund, Par Cornwall E
14. Dellit, Heinz, 28.07.1913, Jena, London E
15. Dienes, Steffen, 04.04.1923, Dresden, London E
16. Dietze, Rudolf Friedrich Gerhart, 02.09.1911, Hamburg, Hamburg -
17. Dippold, Karl, 08.11.1918, Hamburg, Hamburg -
18. Dobrin, Hans, 25.08.1893, Berlin, London E
19. Erbert, Richard Wilhelm/Kleinschmidt, 31.07.1884, Stolzeman, West Byfleet E
20. Erdmann, Hugo, 20.09.1903, Hamburg, Stellingen -
21. Eschborn, Josef Erwin, 11.07.1904, Freiburg, Farnworth E
22. Feinler, Erwin, 01.10.1908, Berlin, Berlin -
23. Feilitz, Adolf, 15.10.1909, Lindow, Hamburg -
24. Finkelstein, Alexis Samuel, 25.01.1877, Leipzig, Cheltenham E
25. Fleischer, Hugo K. H. Albert, 26.02.1913, Köln, Huddersfield E

26. Frank, Julius, 10.04.1891, Zeilitzheim, London E
27. Fromeyer, Anton, 04.05.1907, Thorn, Johannesburg –
28. Gellert Rudolf, 08.08.1922, Glevertz Slesia, London E
29. Gieske, Werner, 08.10.1912, Berlin, Cirencester E
30. Gottfeld, Heinz, 08.02.1907, Bad Polzin, Barranquilla -
31. Graboski, Hans Israel, 08.08.1910, Berlin, Cardiff W
32. Grebe, Otto, 05.09.1914, Klotzen, Essen -
33. Gremme, Heinrich Walter, 03.02.1902, Bochum, Hamburg -
34. Groskopf, Walter, 18.03.1890, Lubben, Buenos Aires -
35. Guhl, Karl, 04.05.1889, Spandau, Hove E
36. Hartmann, Rudolf Gerhardt, 20.09.1913, Stuttgart, Ascot E
37. Heinsohn, Walter, 25.10.1899, Hamburg, Hamburg -
38. Heyland, Alfred Carl, 23.07.1885, Düsseldorf, London E
39. Hirschfeld, Max, 13.03.1889, Berlin, London E
40. Hoene, Karl Albrecht, 09.12.1914, Berlin, London E
41. Jobus, Hero, 05.02.1897, Theringsfen, Theringsfen -
42. Kastner, Herbert, 19.07.1913, Dohna, Dohna -
43. Kirst, Frantisek, 22.06.1907, Berlin, London E
44. Klotzkowsky, Valentin Julius A., 23.09.1896, Nikolaiken, Hamburg -
45. Korner, Rolf Rudolf, 21.08.1908, München Gladbach, London E
46. Krain, Werner Kurt Siegfried, 20.10.1913, Berlin, London E
47. Lamberty, Conrad, 07.04.1866, Aachen, London E
48. Langheck, Heinrich Christian, 20.06.1897, Esslingen, London E
49. Lauscher, Wilhelm, 04.03.1892, Aachen, Leeds E
50. Lessmeister, Emil, 21.03.1884, Hutschenbausen, Nürnberg -
51. Letzke, Johann, 21.01.1877, Krefeld, Macclesfield E
52. Leutelt, Rudolf, 11.06.1907, Innsbruck, Starnberg München -
53. Linke, Wilhelm, 07.05.1907, Hamburg, Celcher -
54. Lissauer, Frido, 12.09.1891, Hamburg London E
55. Loeb, Richard Hermann, 20.03.1902, München, Liverpool E
56. Luetke, Friedrich Anton, 16.03.1912, Barmen, Leicester E
57. Luppe, Gustav Wilhelm H. K., 06.01.1903, Kiel, München -
58. Mai, Richard Willy, 22.06.1910, Oberlungwitz, Mansfield E
59. Mai, Richard Willy, 29.01.1886, Oberlungwitz, Mansfield E
60. Marcus, Fritz, 19.02.1889, Münster, London E

61. Meier, Karl, 25.05.1887, Königstein, Birkenhead E
62. Melchior, Reinhart, 24.03.1921, Charlottenburg, Loughborough E
63. Meyer, Willy C. W., 20.09.1898, Richmond, Surrey, London E
64. Michaelis, Gustav, 09.09.1884, Bruhesdorf, London E
65. Moeller, Hans, 21.08.1912, Bremen, London E
66. Moll, Curt, 10.06.1876, Breslau, London E
67. Moser, Hernst Israel, 27.10.1889, Aachen, Wilmslow E
68. Moser, Karl Friedrich, 27.05.1910, Denzlingen, Denzlingen -
69. Moszkowski, Walter Israel, 28.05.1877, Breslau, London E
70. Mueller, Karl Louis, 07.01.1896, Geestemünde, Bremen -
71. Nagoschiner, Leopold Israel, 11.01.1903, Berlin, London E
72. Neumann, Wilhelm G. Israel, 22.03.1911, Berlin, London E
73. Neumann, Alfred, 05.01.1882, Vienna, London E
74. Olbrisch, Karl, 24.11.1902, Essen, Horsham E
75. Oppers, Emanuel Edward, 25.06.1890, Hanover, Surbiton E
76. Paffen, Gottfried Joseph, 29.11.1882, Aachen, London E
77. Pape, Albert Friedrich, 21.12.1911, Essen, London E
78. Pelzer, Aegidius, 02.04.1912, Köln, Berlin -
79. Peters, Karl, 01.03.1891, Thieds-Bei-Braunschweig, Isleworth E
80. Petersen, Karl, 18.09.1898, Steinfeld, Reykjavile -
81. Plath, Karl Emanuel Gottfried, 17.08.1874, Recklinghausen, London E
82. Reichardt, Rudolf Hermann, 24.03.1915, Pleissa, Cardiff W
83. Repenning, Emil Fritz, 23.02.1880, Kiel, Kiel -
84. Ritterfeld, Karl Heinz, 21.08.1917, Bremen, Bremen -
85. Rossman, Hugo, 03.05.1921, Graz, Graz -
86. Rostin, Walter, 12.04.1899, Charlottenburg, London E
87. Schiffer, Hans Joachim, 16.06.1893, Berlin, Edgware E
88. Schild, Heinz, 14.10.1918, Berlin, London E
89. Schild, Ludwig, 27.02.1891, Magdeburg, London E
90. Schoenthal, Justus Israel, 27.02.1888, Nürnberg, Cumberland E
91. Schreiber, Heinrich Johanne, 14.12.1885, Crombach, Manchester E
92. Schuldt, Hans, 10.05.1901, Kiel, Wustrow Mecklbg. -
93. Schulze, Bruno Friedrich, 27.03.1885, Leipzig, Leipzig -
94. Schutt, Hans Gunther Christian, 08.03.1913, Bergedorf, Middlesex E

95. Schwengeer, Oscar Oswald Otto, 21.09.1879, Berlin, Stockport E
96. Sengebusch, Rudolf, 21.07.1913, Hamburg, Lagos -
97. Siems, Hans Christian Carl, 22.09.1879, Lübeck, London E
98. Sittner, Friedrich, 29.05.1915, Berlin, Loughborough E
99. Steinbruckner, Hans, 02.06.1912, Jena, London E
100. Stern, Ewald Israel, 22.07.1900, Czernowicz, London E
101. Strommer, Nikolaus, 04.12.1904, Miskolecz, London E
102. Thurecht, Walter Alfred, 07.04.1902, Krefeld, Bournemouth E
103. Troetzer, Walter, 05.08.1919, Duisberg, Surbiton E
104. Ultsch, Hans, 09.12.1902, Leipzig, München -
105. Waldowsky, Max William, 30.04.1892, Münster, Warwick E
106. Waldstaedt, Harold Von, 18.02.1899, Heidelberg, Wesermünde -
107. Walter, Christian Frederick, 30.12.1884, Bretzfeld, Stockport E
108. Weber, Lorenz, 19.04.1911, München, London E
109. Weidlich, Paul Emil, 05.06.1876, Brunndobra-Saxony, Macclesfield
    E
110. Weil, Wilhelm Ludwig, 27.10.1914, Frankenthal, London E
111. Weiss, Julius Hermann, 07.11.1865, Stuttgart, London E
112. Wiese, Karl, 29.10.1872, ?, Hamburg -
113. Wilmoswsky, Kurt Freiherr Von, 16.05.1916, Essen-Hügel,
    Naumburg-Saale-Land -
114. Wirth, Eberhard Leo, 15.12.1906, München, Salzach-Oberbayern -
115. Wist, Artur, 20.03.1913, Hamburg, Hamburg -
116. Wohlleten, Hermann Erich, 16.11.1905, Bremen, Accra -
117. Zimmerman, Karl, 26.12.1912, Königsteele, Oberhausen -

Courtesy of Maria Serena Balestracci

Appendix IV

Arandora Star: Missing person list Austrian

Surname and Christian name, D.O.B., Birth Place, Last place of residence

1. Beck, Heinrich Ernst, 26.01.1898, Zborowitz, Newcastle-on-Tyne E
2. Beck, Ludwig Franz, 13.11.1895, Vienna, Northampton E
3. Blumens, Samuel Sigfried, 13.01. 1893, Neumarket, London E
4. Dangl, Erich, 18.02.1910, Waidhofen, A.B.TL Cambridge E
5. Gasteiner, Hermann, 14.01.1908, St. Veit, Hamburg -
6. Glaser, Alexander Israel, 10.07.1909, Vienna, London E
7. Glucksmann, Rubin, 19.05.1889, Czernowitz, London E
8. Gumplowicz, Eduard Ferdinand, 15.05.1923, Vienna, Parkstone E
9. Haupt, Gustav Alfred, 15.09.1910, Seiten-Schweiz, Wersenthal -
10. Hebelka, Ferdinand, 21.05.1897, Vienna, Fenham Newcastle E
11. Hochmann-Littmann, Solomon, 22.02.1907, Kalusz, London E
12. Holdengraber, Friedrich, 23.01.1903, Vienna, London E
13. Holmes, Heinrich Gustav A., 27.09.1922, Vienna, London E
14. Jam, Mor, 30.06.1893, Budafok, London E
15. Kuback, Richard, 23.03.1905, Vienna, London E
16. Neufeld, Fritz, 14.03.1907, Vienna, London E
17. Raab, Fritz, 06.11.1895, Vienna, London E
18. Reichen-Berger, Harry M., 31.07.1896, Vienna, London E
19. Schenk, Rudolph, 08.04.1912, Vienna, Bodrean E
20. Schlamowicz, Fritz, 27.09.1908, Vienna, London E
21. Selka, Paul Erich, 18.05.1919, Vienna, London E
22. Spitzer, Robert, 14.06.1900, Vienna, London E
23. Stoeppel, Heinrich Walter, 28.08.1879, Danzig, London E
24. Toth, Rudolf, 22.10.1911, Guntramsdorf, Sidcup E

Courtesy of Maria Serena Balestracci

Appendix V

Arandora Star: Missing person list Nationality

Unknown

Surname and Christian name, D.O.B, Birth Place, Last place of residence

1. Drews, Emil, 06.04.1897, Danzig/Berlin?, Danzig -
2. Hermann, Simon, 24.06.1892, Stateless, Varshen, Leeds E
3. Hildesheim, Frank Sigmund, 20.03.1876, British, Glasgow, Marlborough, Wilts E
4. Meyer, Ernst Gustav, 23.02.1879, Stateless, Muhliradlitz Slesia, London E
5. Plischke, Richard, 26.07.1889, Czecho-S., Liberec, London E

Courtesy of Maria Serena Balestracci

Appendix VI

Arandora Star: Missing presumed drowned British

Crew

Rank, Name and Surname, Age, Birth Place

1. Chief Steward, Percival Frederick Abbott, 52, Southampton
2. Assistant Steward, Abraham Abrahams, 25, Liverpool
3. Assistant Cook, Henry Lawrence Bache, 59, Liverpool
4. Greaser, George Lowrie Bell, 57, North Shields
5. Assistant Steward, Herbert Leslie Bleasdale, 32, Birkenhead
6. Boatswain's Mate, Joseph Brindley, 37, London
7. Writer, Denis Brook, 20, London
8. Assistant Pantryman, William Ellis Castell, 19, Liverpool
9. Purser, Harold Clegg, 42, London
10. Steward, Robert Charles Cousins, 59, London
11. Fireman, B. Darracotte, 52, Liverpool
12. Pantry Boy, Henry Davies, 18, Liverpool
13. Assistant Steward, Frederick John Edgecombe, 34, Plymouth
14. Assistant Steward, Thomas Ellis, 49, Liverpool
15. Assistant Steward, J. Farquhar, 20, Lerwick
16. Steward's Boy, J. Firth, 18, Birmingham
17. Chief Officer, Hubert Henry Grace, 51, Sheffield
18. Scullion, Jack Almo Halson, 19, Portsmouth
19. Assistant Baker, William Thomas Halson, 28, Portsmouth
20. Donkeyman, George Hamilton, 57, South Shields
21. First Radio Officer, Charles Harris, 46, Peterborough
22. Assistant Pantryman, William James Haslam, 20, Liverpool
23. Assistant Steward, Wilfred Ernest Hayles, 20, Isle of Wight
24. Assistant Steward, Frank Emil William Hobden, 27, Worthing25.
Assistant Steward, Francis Edward Holohan, 51, Kilkenny
26. Assistant Purser, George Pinkerton Hughes, 26, Belfast
27. Writer, Alfred Charles Hutton, 34, London

28. Assistant Steward, Christian Laurits Jacobson, 46, Denmark
29. Able seaman, John Morris Jones, 49, Liverpool
30. Fireman, Richard Kehoe, 52, Wexford
31. Assistant Steward, David Kelleher, 59, Limerick
32. Sailor, Leonard Ernest King, 18, Southampton
33. Second Radio Office, Douglas Bernard Kirkham, 28, Stourbridge
34. Able Seaman, John Joseph Kyte, 59, Liverpool
35. Quartermaster, James Thomas Laurenson, 21, Lerwick
36. Fourth Officer, Ralph Liddle, 27, Essex
37. Assistant Steward, Ronald MacDonald, 35, Fort William
38. Assistant Steward, Patrick Henry Pearse McNally, 22, Belfast
39. Greaser, James McNamee, 57, South Shields
40. Watchman, William Charles Moitie, 60, Jersey
41. Master, Edgar Wallace Moulton, 54, Liverpool
42. Fourth Engineer Officer, Alistair Richard Mowat, 31, New Zealand
43. Fourth Engineer Officer, John Griffiths Mulcahy, 28, Brisbane
44. Scullion, Gerald George Mulvey, 25, Dublin
45. Fireman, Edward Murphy, 53, New Zealand
46. Scullion, Karl Pontus, 22, South Shields
47. Assistant Pantryman, John Patrick Quinn, 39, Worcestershire
48. Second Officer, Stanley Ranson, 40, Liverpool
49. Plumber, Thomas Ferguson Robson, 22, Liverpool
50. Pantryman, Reginald Mathew Sharpe, 36, Southampton
51. Greaser, Rocco Sinacola, 23, London
52. Cook, Gilbert Lawton Smith, 55, Liverpool
53. Fireman, Walter Varley Standing, 49, Toronto
54. Assistant Pantryman, Charles Gordon Stewart, 22, London
55. Assistant Baker, George Allan Watson, 55, Hull
56. Senior Ass Eng Officer, Robert John Wiggins, 24, Monmouthshire
57. Chief Butcher, John Henry Williams, 56, Liverpool
58. Steward, Albert Edward Young, 39, London

Courtesy of Maria Serena Balestracci

Appendix VII

Arandora Star: British Military Guards

Number, Rank, Name and Surname, Age, Regiment

558173, Trooper, Arthur Richard Abbotts, 19, Royal Armoured Corps, Staffordshire Yeomanry

556505, Gunner, Albert William Allison, 23, Royal Artillery, 102 [Northumberland Hussars]

4035427, Private, Geoffrey James Barnett, 27, 4th Bn. Welch Regiment

2984552, Private, Thomas Barr, 26, 5th Bn. Argyll and Sutherland Highlanders

S/159411, Corporal, Leslie Sidney Barrett, 22, Royal Army Service Corps

5620565, Private, Clifford Frederick Bartlett, 20, 4th Bn. Devonshire Regiment

326823, Gunner, William Edward Bates, 38, Royal Artillery, 77 [Duke of Lancaster's Own Yeomanry]

5990254, Private, Herbert John Beckley, 19, 2nd Bn. Hertfordshire Regiment

326536, Trooper, Ronald Joseph Bee, 20, Royal Armoured Corps, Nottinghamshire Yeomanry

5624085, Private, Alfred Henry Beer, 23, 5th Bn. Devonshire Regiment

5614593, Private, John Morton Bedlam, 35, 1st Bn. Devonshire Regiment

4935, Major, Christopher Aleck Bethell, 48, Royal Tank Regiment, Royal Armoured Corps

5990106, Private, Alfred Joseph Birtchnell, 20, 2nd Bn. Hertfordshire Regiment

4126390, Private, Kenneth Philips Blackmore, 21, 7th Bn. Devonshire Regiment

557029, Trooper, James Blundred, 20, Royal Armoured Corps, Staffordshire Yeomanry

3961176, Private, Henry George Brocklebank, 27, 2/5th Bn. Welch Regiment

7178754, C.S.M., David Browne, 35, 9th Bn. Royal Warwickshire Regiment

2977971, Private, Robert Burrell, 29, 5th Bn. Argyll and Sutherland Highlanders

314715, Trooper, George William Buss, 41, Royal Scots Greys [2nd Dragoons]

555851, Gunner, Thomas William Canterford, 23, Royal Artillery

406216, Trooper, Frank Sidney Carter, 27, Royal Armoured Corps, Royal Dragoons

98219, Lt [QM], Thomas Cartman, 47, General List

5726589, Private, William Frederick George Chick, 19, 4th Bn. Dorsetshire Regiment

5619912, Private, Peter Clarke, 17, 4th Bn. Devonshire Regiment

409839, Trooper, William Colquhoun, 21, Lovat Scouts

318740, Trooper, John Connelly, 21, Lovat Scouts

325094, Gunner, Alexander Cuthbert, 20, Royal Artillery

S/149732, Private, Stanley Alfred John Darnell, 25, Royal Army Service Corps

4033447, Private, Clive Darrall, 25, 4th Bn. Welch Regiment

3966070, Private, Charles David, 23, 2/5th Bn. Welch Regiment

554079, Gunner, Leslie Dawson, 26, Royal Artillery, 102 [Northumberland Hussars]

3964603, Private, Donald Ernest Vere Domican, 21, 5th Bn. Welch Regiment

4911816, Corporal, Charles Henry Edgington, 27, Royal Armoured Corps, 1st Bn. Royal Dragoons

5619428, Private, Jack Alva Edmonds, 30, 4th Bn. Devonshire Regiment

5619731, Privat, Richard Wilfred Ellis, 23, 7th Bn. Devonshire Regiment

3958788, Private, Alfred Robert Evans, 24, 4th Bn. Welch Regiment

3955542, Sergeant, Morgan Evans, 31, 2nd Bn. Hertfordshire Regiment

556746, Trooper, Albert Freeman, 31, Royal Armoured Corps, Nottinghamshire Yeomanry

4126237, Private, Sidney Frederick Arthur German,?, 7th Bn. Devonshire Regiment

5623870, Private, Victor Basil Gibbons, 23, 7th Bn. Devonshire Regiment

562337, Private, John Frederick Glanfield, 24, Devonshire Regiment

2981151, Corporal, William Glen, 22, 5th Bn. Argyll and Sutherland Highlanders

49339, Captain, Richard Henry Goddard, 46, 2nd Bn. Middlesex Regiment

5727272, Private, Robert Charles Godfree, 21, 4th Bn. Dorsetshire Regiment

318520, Gunner, Wallace Goodwin, 22, Royal Artillery, 153 [Leicestershire Yeomanry]

323716, Trooper, Robert Grant, 38, Lovat Scouts

406037, Trooper, James Grieve, 37, Lovat Scouts

3963640, Private, Benjamin Griffiths, 33, 4th Bn. Welch Regiment

5623366, Private, Albert Richard John Hannaford, 21, Devonshire Regiment

403988, Trooper, Frank Clifford Harley, 30, Royal Armoured Corps, 1st Royal Dragoons

324110, Trooper, James William Hayles, 28, Yorkshire Dragoons Yeomanry [Queens Own]

3966133, Private, Harry Albert Holmes, 21, 2/5th Bn. Welch Regiment

5989833, Corporal, Harry Holt, 31, 2nd Bn. Hertfordshire Regiment

5624350, Private, Albert Ernest Hudson, 23, 4th Bn. Devonshire Regiment

5990188, Private, Robert Edward Humphreys, 19, 2nd Bn. Hertfordshire Regiment

5951293, Private, John Rylatt Jackson, 22, 2nd Bn. Hertfordshire Regiment

3963326, Private, William Samuel John, 21, 4th Bn. Welch Regiment

318248, Gunner, John Johnson, 27, Royal Artillery

3963311, Private, Oliver Jones, 36, 4th Bn. Welch Regimen

3966164, Private, William John Jones, 22, 2/5th Bn. Welch Regiment

5723819, Sapper, Frederick Charles Kellaway, 27, Royal Engineers

322429, Trooper, Norman James King, ?, Warwickshire Yeomanry

5619142, Private, Edward George Lane, 21, 7th Bn. Devonshire Regiment

5989119, Private, Osmund Thomas Langley, 25, 2nd Bn. Hertfordshire Regiment

7562775, Gunner, Edward Macon, 34, Royal Artillery

322158, Gunner, James McKenna, 30, Royal Artillery, 155 [Lanarkshire Yeomanry]

112773, Lieut., Edward Sydney William Miles, 45, 7th Bn. King's Royal Rifle Corps

5623901, Private, Owen Mitchell, 23, 7th Bn. Devonshire Regiment

317969, Gunner, Thomas Dunn Moore, 23, Royal Artillery, 155 [Lanarkshire Yeomanry]

558176, Trooper, Thomas Mullis, 19, Royal Armoured Corps, Staffs Yeomanry

326063, Trooper, Frank Geoffrey Munton, 24, Yorkshire Hussars Yeomanry

325618, Gunner, John Frederick Murphy, 23, Royal Artillery, 77 [Duke of Lancaster's Own Yeomanry]

4688185, Trooper, George Haller Newcombe, 25, Royal Armoured Corps, Queen's Own Yorkshire Dragoons

5989692, Private, James Thomas Oakley, 25, 2nd Bn. Hertfordshire Regiment

5612172, Private, Francis Percy Palmer, 35, 7th Bn. Devonshire Regiment

5718142, CQMS, Harry Gordon Payne, 48, Somerset Light Infantry

3962740, Private, Maldwyn Phillips, 20, 2/5th Bn. Welch Regt

362437, Gunner, Francis Charles Price, 26, Royal Artillery, 75 [Shropshire Yeomanry]

3952211, Private, David Thomas Rees, 36, 4th Bn. Welch Regiment

5990162, Private, Harold Alfred Robins, 20, 2nd Bn. Hertfordshire Regiment

2817123, Trooper, William Urquhart Ross, 28, Lovat Scouts

5621426, Private, Cecil Arthur St. John-Clifford, 27, 7th Bn. Devonshire Regiment

5614987, Private, Percival George Sampson, 32, 7th Bn. Devonshire Regiment

5619117, Corporal, Roy James Skerrett, 20, 7th Bn. Devonshire Regiment

406316, Trooper, William Smith, 28, Royal Armoured Corps, 1st Royal Dragoons

326332, Gunner, Alfred Nigel Whitley Sykes, 21, Royal Artillery, 75 [Shropshire Yeomanry]

3248098, Rifleman, Peter Lluellyn Gordon Tarchetti, 31, 9th Bn. Cameronians [Scottish Rifles]

5990119, Private, Henry Ronald Taylor, 19, 2nd Bn. Hertfordshire Regiment

5726643, Private, Ronald Walter Terrell, 20, 4th Bn. Dorsetshire Regiment

318656, Trooper, Herschell Thompson, 35, Yorkshire Dragoons Yeomanry [Queens Own]

5990284, Private, Frederick William Wells, 22, 2nd Bn. Hertfordshire Regiment

325208, Trooper, Alexander Wilson, 34, Lovat Scouts

3247652, Rifleman, John Wilson, 26, 9th Bn. Cameronians [Scottish Rifles]

5621415, Corporal, Douglas James Wyatt, 22, 7th Bn. Devonshire Regiment

CH/20011, Marine, Ernest Edward Warren, 44, Royal Marines, HMS President 111

Courtesy of Maria Serena Balestracci

Notes

Chapter 1

1. Transcription of author interview, Graziella Feraboli, Milan, 22.08.07
2. Transcription of author interview, Graziella Feraboli, Milan, 22.08.07
3. Transcription of author interview, Frank Longinotti, Lancashire, 25.07.08
4. Transcription of author interview, Joe Pieri, Glasgow, 02.12.06
5. Transcription of author interview, Clementina Cordani, Wales, 22.03.07

Chapter 2

1. Transcription of author interview, Peter Foster, Huntingdon, 20.11.07
2. Transcription of author interview, Graziella Feraboli, Milan, 22.08.07
3. Transcription of author interview, Graziella Feraboli, Milan, 22.08.07
4. Transcription of author interview, Bruna Bonino, London, 19.08.07
5. Transcription of author interview, Frank Longinotti, Lancashire, 25.07.08
6. Transcription of author Interview, Armo Collini, London, 21.01.07

Chapter 3

1. Transcription of author interview, Graziella Feraboli, Milan, 22.08.07
2. Transcription of author interview, Albert Cavalli, London, 04.05.05
3. Transcription of author interview, Rita Pezzani, London, 21.08.07
4. Transcription of author interview, Graziella Feraboli, Milan, 22.08.07

Chapter 4

1. Transcription of author interview, Rupert Limentani, Milan, 07.10.07
2. *Daily Mirror*, 27 April 1940, cited in Colpi, Terri (1991) *The Italian Factor: The Italian Community in Great Britain*, Edinburgh: Mainstream Publishing Company
3. W. Churchill, Hansard 13 May 1940

Chapter 5

1. Transcription of author interview, Bruna Bonino, London, 19.08.07
2. Transcription of author interview, Aurelio Tarquini, London, 10.06.05
3. Transcription of author interview, Clementina Cordani, Wales, 22.03.07

4. Transcription of author interview, Joe Pieri, Glasgow, 02.12.06

5. Transcription of author interview, Joe Pieri, Glasgow, 02.12.06

6. Transcription of author interview, Fosca Rendina, London, 13.09.07

7. Transcription of author interview, Rita Pezzani, London, 21.08.07

8. Transcription of author interview, Aurelio Tarquini, London, 10.06.05

9. Aliens Protected Orders Letter

Chapter 6

1. Transcription of author interview, Graziella Feraboli, Milan, 22.08.07

2. Transcription of author interview, Graziella Feraboli, Milan, 22.08.07

3. Transcription of author interview, Joe Pieri, Glasgow, 02.12.06

4. Transcription of author interview, Rando Bertoia, Glasgow, 22.12.05

5. Transcription of author interview, Maria Moruzzi, London, 12.03.07

6. Transcription of author interview, Clementina Cordani, Wales, 22.03.07

7. Transcription of author interview, Bruna Bonino, London, 19.08.07

8. Transcription of author interview, Aurelio Tarquini, London, 10.06.05

9. Transcription of author interview, Joe Pieri, Glasgow, 02.12.06

10. Transcription of author interview, Albert Cavalli, London, 04.05.05

11. Transcription of author interview, Albert Cavalli, London, 04.05.05

Chapter 7

1. Transcription of author interview, Dino Viazzani, Bardi, 02.07.07

2. Transcription of author interview, Graziella Feraboli, Milan, 22.08.07

3. *Bury Times*, 15 June 1940

4. *Bury Times*, 15 June 1940

5. *Bury Times*, 15 June 1940

6. Transcription of author interview, Joe Pieri, Glasgow, 02.12.06

7. Transcription of author interview, Joe Pieri, Glasgow, 02.12.06

8. Transcription of author interview, Dino Viazzani, Bardi, 02.07.07

9. Transcription of author interview, Graziella Feraboli, Milan, 22.08.07

Chapter 8

1. Transcription of author interview, Rita Pezzani, London, 21.08.07
2. Transcription of author interview, Joe Pieri, Glasgow, 02.12.06
3. Transcription of author interview, Rando Bertoia, Glasgow, 22.12.05

Chapter 9

1. Transcription of author interview, Dino Viazzani, Bardi, 02.07.07
2. Transcription of author interview, Albert Cavalli, London, 04.05.05
3. Transcription of author interview, Albert Cavalli, London, 04.05.05
4. Transcription of author interview, Vito Maestranzi, London, 14.03.07
5. Transcription of author interview, Dino Viazzani, Bardi, 02.07.07
6. Transcription of author interview, Albert Cavalli, London, 04.05.05
7. Transcription of author interview, Clementina Cordani, Wales, 22.03.07
8. Transcription of author interview, Bruna Bonino, London, 19.08.07
9. Transcription of author interview, Bruna Bonino, London, 19.08.07

10. Transcription of author interview, Aurelio Tarquini, London, 10.06.05

11. Transcription of author interview, Alfred Tisi, London, 11.09.07

12. Transcription of author interview, Vito Maestranzi, London, 14.03.07

13. Transcription of author interview, Dino Viazzani, Bardi, 02.07.07

14. Transcription of author interview, Clementina Cordani, Wales, 22.03.07

Chapter 10

1. Transcription of author interview, Joe Pieri, Glasgow, 02.12.06

2. Transcription of author interview, Joe Pieri, Glasgow, 02.12.06

3. Transcription of author interview, Dino Viazzani, Bardi, 02.07.07

4. Transcription of author interview, Rupert Limentani, Milan, 07.10.07

5. Transcription of author interview, Joe Pieri, Glasgow, 02.12.06

6. Transcription of author interview, Rupert Limentani, Milan, 07.10.07

7. Transcription of author interview, Rando Bertoia, Glasgow, 22.12.05

8. Transcription of author interview, Harold Finney, Stoke-on-Trent, 15.04.07

9. Transcription of author interview, Rupert Limentani, Milan, 07.10.07

10. WO 361/4

Chapter 11

1. Transcription of author interview, Harold Finney, Stoke-on-Trent, 15.04.07

2. Transcription of author interview, Harold Finney, Stoke-on-Trent, 15.04.07

3. Transcription of author interview, Harold Finney, Stoke-on-Trent, 15.04.07

4. Transcription of author interview, Rando Bertoia, Glasgow, 22.12.05

5. Transcription of author interview, Rupert Limentani, Milan, 07.10.07

6. Letter from Angela Albericci daughter of Angelo Albericci dated 21 March
    2007

7. Transcription of author interview, Rupert Limentani, Milan, 07.10.07

8. ADM 199/141

Chapter 12

1. Transcription of author interview, Rando Bertoia, Glasgow, 22.12.05

2. Transcription of author interview, Rupert Limentani, Milan, 07.10.07

3. Transcription of author interview, Rando Bertoia, Glasgow, 22.12.05
4. ADM 199/141
5. Letter from Angela Albericci, daughter of Angelo Albericci, dated 21 March
2007
6. ADM 199/141

Chapter 13

1. Transcription of author interview, Graziella Feraboli, Milan, 22.08.07
2. *Daily Telegraph*, 4 July 1940
3. *Daily Telegraph*, 4 July 1940
4. Transcription of author interview, Graziella Feraboli, Milan, 22.08.07
5. Transcription of author interview, Graziella Feraboli, Milan, 22.08.07
6. Transcription of author interview, Liliana Cortesio, London 09.09.05
7. Transcription of author interview, Clementina Cordani, Wales, 22.03.07
8. H/O letter to Cortesio House
9. Home Office 213/1834, 'Sinking of the "Arandora Star"', Lord Snell's report
10. Home Office 214/3, 'Del Grosso Giuseppe'
11. Home Office 214/3, 'Del Grosso Giuseppe'
12. Transcription of author interview, Rupert Limentani, Milan, 07.10.07

13. Letter from Angela Albericci, daughter of Angelo Albericci, dated 21 March 2007

Chapter 14

1. Transcription of author interview, Joe Pieri, Glasgow, 02.12.06
2. Transcription of author interview, Joe Pieri, Glasgow, 02.12.06
3. Transcription of author interview, Joe Pieri, Glasgow, 02.12.06
4. Transcription of author interview, Joe Pieri, Glasgow, 02.12.06
5. Transcription of author interview, Joe Pieri, Glasgow, 02.12.06
6. Transcription of author interview, Joe Pieri, Glasgow, 02.12.06
7. Transcription of author interview, Maria Moruzzi, London, 12.03.07
8. Transcription of author interview, Rando Bertoia, Glasgow, 22.12.05
9. Transcription of author interview, Rando Bertoia, Glasgow, 22.12.05
10. Transcription of author interview, Rando Bertoia, Glasgow, 22.12.05

Chapter 15

1. Transcription of author interview, Dino Viazzani, Bardi, 02.07.07
2. Transcription of author interview, Albert Cavalli, London, 04.05.05
3. Transcription of author interview, Albert Cavalli, London, 04.05.05
4. Transcription of author interview, Albert Cavalli, London, 04.05.05
5. Transcription of author interview, Joe Pieri, Glasgow, 02.12.06
6. Transcription of author interview, Joe Pieri, Glasgow, 02.12.06
7. Transcription of author interview, Rando Bertoia, Glasgow, 22.12.05

Chapter 16

1. Transcription of author interview, Liliana Cortesio, London 09.09.05
2. Transcription of author interview, Rupert Limentani, Milan, 07.10.07
3. Transcription of author interview, Harold Finney, Stoke-on-Trent, 15.04.07
4. Transcription of author interview, Rando Bertoia, Glasgow, 22.12.05
5. WO 361/4

6. Transcription of author interview, Joe Pieri, Glasgow, 02.12.06

7. Transcription of author interview, Rando Bertoia, Glasgow, 22.12.05

8. Transcription of author interview, Graziella Feraboli, Milan, 22.08.07

Chapter 17

1. *Manchester Guardian*, 21 March 1941

2. St Peters Church, Clerkenwell

3. Transcription of author interview, Graziella Feraboli, Milan, 22.08.07

4. Transcription of author interview, Graziella Feraboli, Milan, 22.08.07

Bibliography

Balestracci, S.M. (2008) *Arandora Star: From Oblivion to Memory*, Fidenza: Monte Universita Parma

Bosworth, R.J.B. (2002) *Mussolini*, London: Arnold

Bungay, Stephen. (2001) *The Most Dangerous Enemy: A History of the Battle of Britain*, London: Aurum Press Ltd

Frank, Wolfgang (1954) *Enemy Submarine: The Exploits of the U-Boat Captain Who Penetrated Scapa Flow*, London: William Kimber and Co. Ltd

Ceserani, D. & T. Kushner (eds) (1993) *The Internment of Aliens in Twentieth Century Britain*, London: Frank Cass & Company Ltd

Chappell, Connery (2005) *Island of Barbed Wire: The Remarkable Story of World War Two Internment on the Isle of Man*, London: Hale

Churchill, Winston (2002) *The Second World War*, London: Pimlico

Churchill, Winston (2005) *The Gathering Storm: The Second World War Volume 1*, London: Penguin

Churchill, S. Winston (2004) *Never Give In!: The Best of Winston Churchill's Speeches*, London: Pimlico

Colpi, Terri (1991) *The Italian Factor: The Italian Community in Great Britain*, Edinburgh: Mainstream Publishing Company

Colpi, Terri (1991) *Italians Forward: A Visual History of the Italian Community in Great Britain*, Edinburgh: Mainstream Publishing Company

Cooke, Terry (2002) *Little Italy: A History of Liverpool's Italian Community*, Liverpool, The Bluecoat Press

DiStasi, Lawrence (2001) *The Secret History of Italian American Evacuation and Internment During World War 2*, Berkeley, CA: Heyday Books

Davis, Alan (2004) *Colonsay's Fallen*, Isle of Colonsay: Colonsay Books

Dove, Richard (2005) *'Totally Un-English'? Britain's Internment of 'Enemy Aliens' in Two World Wars*, Netherlands: Rodopi

Eden, Sir Anthony (1960) *The Memoirs of Sir Anthony Eden: Full Circle*, London: Cassell & Company Ltd (first published in 1960)

Eden, Sir Anthony (1962) *The Eden Memoirs: Facing the Dictators*, London: Cassell & Company Ltd

Forte, Charles (1986) *The Autobiography of Charles Forte*, London: Pan Books

Gillman, P., & L. Gillman (1980) *'Collar the Lot!' How Britain Interned and Expelled Its Wartime Refugees*, London: Quartet Books Limited

Hughes, Colin (2008) *Lime, Lemon & Sarsaparilla: The Italian Community in SouthWales 1881–1945*, Wales: Seren

Kershaw, R., & M. Pearsall (2004) *Immigrants and Aliens: A Guide to Sources on UK Immigration and Citizenship*, Richmond: The National Archives

Lafitte, François (1988) *The Internment of Aliens*, London: Libris (first published 1940)

Malkin, Michelle (2004) *In Defense of Internment: The Case for 'Racial Profiling' in World War 2 and the War on Terror*, Washington, Regnery Publishing, Inc.

Martin, Sir John (1991) *Downing Street: The War Years*, London: Bloomsbury Publishing Limited

Mark, Sir Robert (1979) *In the Office of Constable: An Autobiography*, Glasgow: William Collins Sons & Co Ltd

Muggeridge, Malcolm (2002) *Ciano's Diary*, London: Phoenix Press

Pieri, Joe (1997) *Isle of the Displaced: An Italian-Scot's Memoirs of Internment in the Second World War*, Glasgow: Neil Wilson Publishing Ltd

Pieri, Joe (2006) *The Scots-Italians: Recollections of an Immigrant*, Edinburgh: Mercat Press Ltd

Pieri, Joe (2006) *River of Memory: Memoirs of a Scots-Italian*, Edinburgh: Mercat Press Ltd

Roberts, Frank (1991) *Dealing with Dictators: The Destruction and Revival of Europe 1930–70*, London: George Weidenfeld & Nicolson Ltd

Schull, Joseph (1991) *Far Distant Ships: An Official Account of Canadian Naval Operations in World War 2*, Toronto: Stoddard Publishing Co. Limited

Stent, Ronald (1980) *A Bespattered Page? The Internment of 'His Majesty's most Loyal Enemy Aliens'*, London: André Deutch Ltd

Tennent, J. Alan (2002) *British and Commonwealth Merchant Ship Losses To Axis Submarines 1939–1945*, Stroud: Sutton Publishing Ltd